Happy Holidays
from
The 5th Avenue
Club

EXTRAORDINARY JEWELS

JOHN TRAINA

Extraordinary Jewels

FOREWORD BY DANIELLE STEEL

DOUBLEDAY

NEW YORK LONDON TORONTO SYDNEY AUCKLAND

PUBLISHED BY DOUBLEDAY
a division of Bantam Doubleday Dell Publishing Group, Inc.
1540 Broadway, New York, New York 10036

DOUBLEDAY and the portrayal of an anchor with a dolphin are
trademarks of Doubleday, a division of
Bantam Doubleday Dell Publishing Group, Inc.

Design by Sisco & Evans

Grateful acknowledgment is made to the following:

"Diamonds Are a Girl's Best Friend" from *Gentlemen Prefer Blondes*.
Words by Leo Robin, Music by Jule Styne, Copyright 1949 (Renewed) by Dorsey Bros. Music,
a division of Music Sales Corporation (ASCAP).
International Copyright Secured. All Rights Reserved.
Reprinted by Permission.

Excerpts from *Tiffany Touch* reprinted by permission of Julian Bach Agency.
Copyright © 1971.

Library of Congress Cataloging-in-Publication Data
Traina, John.
Extraordinary jewels / by John Traina. — 1st ed.
p.   cm.
1. Jewelry—History.   2. Jewelers—Biography—History and
criticism.   3. Jewelers—Anecdotes.   I. Title.
NK7306.T73   1994
739.27´09—dc20   93-34454
                                          CIP

ISBN 0-385-26644-8
Copyright © 1994 by John Traina
All Rights Reserved
Printed in the United States of America
September 1994

First Edition
1   3   5   7   9   10   8   6   4   2

COVER PHOTOGRAPH:
*Ruby-and-diamond necklace by Harry Winston, containing 369 diamonds weighing 122.69
carats, and 14 oval Burmese rubies weighing 138.12 carats.
Harry Winston, Inc.*

FRONTISPIECE:
*"The Diamonds of Tiffany" brooch: 51.52 carats of marquise- and pear-shaped diamonds set in platinum,
surrounding a magnificent 107.65-carat fancy yellow diamond set in 18-karat gold. Brooch may also be
worn as a pendant. (Courtesy Tiffany & Co., San Francisco)
Fred Lyon*

For Oyl with love

CONTENTS

Foreword

by Danielle Steel

Jewels . . . fascinating jewels . . . mysterious jewels . . . dazzling . . . opulent . . . extravagant . . . exciting. The words associated with jewelry are almost as mesmerizing as the jewels themselves. The jewels conjure up images of exotic places, diamond mines in Africa, emeralds in Colombia . . . sapphires in Thailand . . . rubies in Burma . . . Ceylon . . . Brazil. The very idea of wringing something so staggeringly beautiful as an emerald, a diamond, a ruby, from the bosom of nature makes one dream.

From the days of King Tut, to the Romans, Etruscans, and Greeks, to the Middle Ages, and the court of Louis XIV, jewels have played an important part in the lives of royals and important people, as well as ordinary mortals like the rest of us. The ancients were buried with them. In more modern times, people have bought them, found them, traded them, sold them, sometimes stolen them, or simply paid a king's ransom for them. But however they acquired them, from a mine, or an auction house, or a jeweler on Fifth Avenue or the Place Vendôme, there is always, always a breathless excitement to their acquisition. People have gotten excited over jewels for centuries, and continue to do so today. They are the badges of the very rich, and the not so very rich, the very ambitious, and the very beautiful. For the just married or just engaged, they adorn, they excite, they seem to cast a spell over giver and receiver, buyer and seller, wearer and observer. Who that has seen Elizabeth Taylor in her spectacular diamonds has not been dazzled by her beauty—and her jewels? Who can ever forget the famous faces known for wearing famous jewels . . . Sophia Loren . . . Merle Oberon . . . the Duchess of Windsor . . . the maharajahs of India . . . empresses and queens and princes, movie stars, or merely beautiful women. All of them enhanced, enlarged, by the jewels they've worn.

Where does the fascination begin? Where does it end? It goes all the way back to ancient times, and before. Nothing excited the world more than the opening of the tomb of King Tutankhamen in 1922. People flocked to see the treasures, as they still do today. As a result, important jewelry in the 1920s was instantly affected by Egyptian designs. The opening of the tomb caused new trends, and new looks in fashion as well as jewels.

Not surprisingly, jewelry and fashion have always gone hand in hand, particularly in the 1930s and '40s, when style seemed all-important, and Paris fashion and haute couture held the world in their thrall. It was a world for only the very rich, yet everyone outside, looking in, loved to watch and even wanted to "copy."

Admiring a pavé-diamond vine-shaped brooch from a duchess's estate in Monte Carlo, Fred Leighton chose to render this new and elegant version of the brooch using carved rock crystal. (Courtesy Fred Leighton)
Andrew Edgar

What were they wearing? What tiara? What gown? What scandal? Whose mistress? What jewels? The jewels were fabulous in those days, accessible primarily to the very wealthy, as they had been for many years.

Turn-of-the-century jewels were fascinating too. Important pieces were worn by important people, with large stones in impressive settings. Collars, chokers, stomachers, tiaras, were the rule, worn by people whose names we've heard, and who conjure up a lost world. It was a world epitomized by those who traveled on the ill-fated *Titanic*. Astors, Wideners, Thayers, people of Boston, Philadelphia, Paris, London, New York. The setters of all trends. They set sail on the ship's maiden voyage, bearing with them endless steamer trucks filled with Paris gowns, and coffers laden with exquisite jewels. The jewels of those days were admittedly quieter than some we see today, due to older styles of cutting the stones, but the stones were large and pure and impressive.

By the 1930s and '40s, though, styles had changed. Jewelry was no longer quite as serious, fashion had become more involved. The large jewelry houses were already well established by then, and setting styles of their own. A fascination with low-cut dresses set the stage for larger, more striking necklaces. Style and jewelers were collaborating, with dazzling results.

Interestingly, before that time, all the way back to the 1850s, it was jewelry, in a sense, which led the style. Jewelry designers were considered artisans of great importance, and jewelry was considered high art. But the 1930s were "modern times," and fashion designers like Coco Chanel were adding a touch of irreverence to jewels as well, sometimes creating real pieces to look like fakes, ropes and ropes of pearls, interspersed with precious jewels. She loved imitating her own real jewelry, and made fabulous imitations of her own well-known Verdura cuffs: beautifully carved bangles of black onyx, each emblazoned with a gold Maltese cross encrusted with precious stones and pearls, now in the possession of Fred Leighton.

People were not afraid to be ostentatious then. On the contrary, people wanted to look rich, and those who could made a point of wearing important jewels. And like the world of high fashion, the world of "high jewelry" was at its finest in France. Nine-tenths of the world's important jewelry houses have been, historically, French. Not surprisingly somehow, the exotic artistry of fine jewelry seems well mastered by the French. There are, and have been, other important jewelers, of course, from different nations (Bulgari, Buccellati, Asprey, Garrard, Tiffany, Winston, Webb, et al.)—but France seems to have garnered most (Van Cleef, Cartier, Mauboussin, Boivin, Belperron, Boucheron, Lalique, et al.).

World War II brought in new and different trends. Suddenly exquisite stones from exotic countries were less readily available, and jewelry designers began to create intriguing alternatives, often using semiprecious stones, or gunmetal rather than gold. Van Cleef & Arpels have always been noted for their impressive work with semiprecious stones, coral, turquoise, amethysts. Seaman Schepps was well known for using semiprecious stones too, as was Fulco di Verdura, and later David Webb. Today, Paloma Picasso creates magic with aquamarines, peridots, kunzite, tanzanite, a rainbow of remarkable hues that offer an interesting alternative to rubies, sapphires, emeralds, and diamonds.

The 1940s and '50s, after the war, became opulent once again. Ostentation was wonderful—show the world that all is well! Women sparkled in remarkable jewels from all the important houses, daring to wear veritable fortunes, in keeping with their important names: Barbara Hutton, Marjorie Merriweather Post, Florence Gould, Elizabeth Taylor, Lana Turner, and Paulette Goddard. Not surprisingly, World War II altered who bought the jewels, and sometimes where they got them. Originally, the most important buyers had always been royals and rulers, and eventually wealthy Europeans and Americans as well. Indian buyers had always been a notable force in the jewelry market, and both Van Cleef & Arpels and Cartier were clever in catering to them with Indian-inspired designs. Today, these pieces are seen in the auction houses with considerable frequency, and at antique stores like Fred Leighton in New York. Great bibs of emeralds, great knobs of rubies, jewels of a size and color and scope that one rarely sees anywhere today. Before the war, these fabulous collections were still being made.

Just after the war, more of the big buyers were from the United States. European buyers were more moderate for a time. And in recent years, the big jewelry buyers have rotated among countries in power, those with great economic strength. Japan, the Arab states, Italy, Germany, some Asian and African countries, and the United States have been the geographic sites during times of prosperity. The computer market has brought fabulous wealth to certain areas, the oil market has brought periods of great fortune to other areas just as coal and ore did in earlier periods. But the United States has had an important place in the jewelry market for a long time, and continues to remain there, although perspectives have sometimes changed. But jewels have continued to be bought, sold, traded, and loved by Americans, and many nations, for a long, long time.

Love of jewelry had a very high point in the 1940s and '50s, with designers creating impressive designs for celebrated people who were not afraid to wear them. Hollywood movie stars began to amass jewels as well. And on the whole, people were willing to look ostentatious in order to look important. Extravagant jewelry was an essential part of that look. By then, jewelry had become far more important than fashion.

The Kennedys brought with them magic and charm and elegance in the 1960s. The idea of an American aristocracy had its place in the world, and along with it style and beauty. Jewelry once again became an integral part of that. And the jewelry of the '60s continues to show a bravery about extravagance, and a look that said fabulous jewels were desirable above all. The Arabs continued to be major buyers then as well. And their fascination with jewelry fascinated those who watched them. The sellers were exotic, the buyers were exotic, the places where they bought jewelry were exotic: Monte Carlo, Paris, Tehran, Geneva, New York, Rome, Hong Kong, Jedda. The places where jewelry is bought and sold continue to lure the very rich, and to be the meccas of where truly gorgeous jewelry is found. There are smaller spots as well . . . St. Moritz, Palm Beach, Cannes, all the haunts of the wealthy and worldly. One can stand and stare, even now, openmouthed, at the extraordinary merchandise in the windows, and the equally extraordinary people who buy it.

Jewelry in the 1970s continued in much the same vein. And then there were the opulent '80s. The Big Time. Big money, big spenders, a lush and lavish world. New cuts of important stones were perfected: the starburst, which sometimes made less exciting stones knock your eyes out with their newfound sparkle. New colors became important as well. Whereas pink and blue and red diamonds had always been held in great esteem, suddenly a variety of yellows became important as well, along with browns, champagne, cognac, and a range of colors that became highly fashionable and brought important sums.

Important sums. One would think that that is the key. But it isn't. That's the amazing thing about jewels. Jewels are romance. Jewels are magic. Jewels are a woman looking at fifty bracelets, a hundred stones, and then hearing her gasp over just one . . . it's a mad piece of jewelry that no one could love . . . but just one woman does . . . it's a battle to the death between two buyers at an auction house, sending prices through the roof. It is *having* to have something that will *never* come again . . . or will it? Has it? Could it be? No . . . each time it's different. It's a kind of love that propels jewelry buyers toward their purchases; not just greed, or a passion for acquisition, it's an absolute love for the stone, the look, the design. It is passion. It is desire. It is all-consuming. Each year, countless stones are bought, traded, sold, exchanged, stolen, taken, coveted, devoured by those who love them, need them, want them, *must* have them.

It is a passion one can only begin to understand while watching an auction, it is a kind of barely controlled, just within polite frenzy of *having* to have whatever is on the auction block at the time. The items are cruised and perused beforehand by aficionados, the knowledgeable and the naive, dealers and private individuals. They are tried on, examined, looked at through loupes, held in warm hands or slipped on cool fingers, silently appraised . . . and then the fight begins. The day comes. The moment arrives . . . the breath is held . . . the hand is raised . . . a tiny discreet sign, a look of intense passion in the eyes . . . voices muffled on dozens of transatlantic calls, a shriek of hysteria, a caller is forgotten somewhere in the world, it can't have happened . . . it can't be . . . but it is . . . the piece is gone forever. Gone to a canny dealer who will price it well, who may already have an anxious buyer among his clientele, or a man or woman who wanted it desperately. There is desperation along with the passion.

Never was this more apparent than at the Sotheby's auction of the jewelry of the Duchess of Windsor. The auction was held in Geneva in 1987 and attended by 2,675 people. Countless bidders waited breathlessly on the phones as the prices soared. Items estimated optimistically at four to six thousand dollars went for four hundred thousand . . . six hundred thousand . . . eight . . . a million. It astounded the eye, it amazed the ear. It boggled the mind. A total of $50,281,887 changed hands for a total of 305 items, some of them very lovely, some of them surprisingly mundane, such as half dress sets for a gentleman, or some very nice Seaman Schepps shell earrings which sold for eighteen times what they would have in the store. Amethysts were sold for the price of flawless diamonds. Buyers went completely mad.

The effect of that sale has been felt long since. Even in a world economy that has shown signs of stress in every possible way, the prices of jewelry at auction have held firm. Auction houses are now seldom the home of a bargain. They are places to find great pieces, but rarely at great prices. The one true boon of auction houses—other than the remarkable wares they offer to a still fascinated world—is the access they have given buyers in distant corners of the world. Their catalogues go everywhere, offering a maharani's collection to buyers halfway around the world. Jewelry is more available today because of the auctions.

But as the '80s gave way to the '90s, times inevitably changed. The world economy suffered, world problems proliferated: unemployment, violence, class issues, racial issues, angry people, poor people, homeless people, sick people, frightened people. Problems that have plagued civilization for years, yet seem to be particularly rampant in the last decade of the twentieth century. Problems which seem to be, for the moment, unresolved. Fear has changed the face of jewelry for now. Styles have changed, fashion has changed dramatically. Fashion is trendy, "punk." In the early '90s, even the distinguished house of Chanel showed the "grunge" look on its runway, a look inspired by the people of the streets. Lavish high fashion and high style have been altered remarkably. Fur is "mock." Real fur has all but disappeared, and with it signs of opulence which are no longer admired, but are used as matches to set to a tinderbox of woes. In South American countries, women carry jewels unobtrusively in paper bags on their way to secretly luxurious parties. In Italy, fashionable aristocratic women wear simple cloth coats, or unexciting raincoats, to cover an array of fabulous jewels and elegant gowns. In many countries, if not most, women are wearing their jewels more privately than ever before, in their homes, in the homes of friends, beneath veils in Arab countries, in privacy, and in secret. But the romance and the fascination are still there. Perhaps even more so. Jewels are still being bought and sold and worn, ogled at auction houses and eyed with envy. It is a passion that will never die.

Through the ages and throughout time, the love of jewels has been there, the fascination with their origins, their owners, their destinations, the dreams they represent. To touch rare and wonderful jewels is to touch a world everyone aspires to, a world of beauty and elegance, a world once owned by the royals . . . it is a peek into a private kingdom, a secret life, an elusive world. To acquire them, to touch them, even to see them, is to drift into a fascinating place. Even today, with far more pressing issues upon us, it is impossible not to be moved by these wonderful jewels, not to be struck by their beauty, awed by all they represent.

The world's love affair with important jewels will live on forever. It defies world events, it surpasses economy and logistics. In truth, it is not the actual value of the jewels which excites. It is their beauty, their mystery, their lure. From King Tut until today, jewels have represented something we all long for, something we would like to have or be, even for a moment in time. Jewels are romance, they are fashion, they are art . . . but more than that, they are magic . . . they are love. Jewels are, far beyond their value, a remarkable gift of nature . . . from God.

Danielle and John.
Roger Ressmeyer, Starlight

Preface

How did my extensive traveling and shopping get started? Early on, I figured out that my father had the money and that my mother had the desire to spend it. The energy and time she was willing to devote to buying, ordering, and being fitted for shoes, furs, gowns, jewels, knew no bounds. She was tireless in her pursuit of perfection. In fact, it took more than energy and money; it took time and the willingness to travel—to Rome for coats, Perugia for knits, Paris for gowns and shoes, London for tweeds, New York for furs, and *everywhere* (Florence, Paris, Rome, the Italian and French Rivieras) for jewels.

In those days you also had to travel to the places where you wore those creations. And to make it more amusing, you had to travel still farther to find the people to impress with the jewels and gowns you were wearing.

My father was long-suffering and stoic about these adventures. But in truth, I think he enjoyed the people, places, and events, and having a beautiful wife beside him. My grandparents, however, were horrified by the extravagance. And for my part, as a child, I found it all incredibly boring and could never understand why you had to go to so much trouble, and so far afield, to buy clothes and wear them. The more mysterious places intrigued me, the ships fascinated me, and jewelry always seemed the most important part of the show to me: The Finale. But in spite of that, I spent a lot of time complaining, as my mother spent hours selecting hats and gowns, the perfect pearls, and the most beautiful earrings.

As a man, I discovered while traveling throughout the world that jewelry was not only interesting to look at and compare, but easy to buy and take with me. Wherever I was, I could buy it, slip it in a pocket with great ease, and take it home to someone. I also discovered early on that jewelry made a much bigger impression on a woman than any other gift I could have brought.

The comparison of outstanding stones, and the recognition of unusual stones and colors, variations of cut and quality, became a fascination to me. And beyond that, as my own knowledge grew, being able to identify designers began to amuse me, not unlike being able to distinguish a Packard from a Buick. Jewelry became a game I could play while I worked, bringing with it unexpected rewards, producing delight and devotion from its recipients.

For thirty years I was able to combine my career in shipping and constant travel with a relentless pursuit of extraordinary stones and unusual jewelry.

Macau.

In some forty trips to Japan, starting at age twenty, I would try to visit the Mikimoto shops in Yokohama, Tokyo, Osaka, Nagoya, Kobe, and Kyoto and slowly work my way from the traditional lustrous, slightly pink strand of pearls to the larger individual pearls. Collections of individual pearls grew with the size of the pearls and gave way to include the baroque and off-color pearls that have now become a more unusual part of today's jewelry. Visiting the pearl divers (or *amas*, as they are called) in Ago Bay and other fishing villages scattered along the Japanese coast, I was able to gain an appreciation for the labor-intensive process that goes into the formation of each and every pearl cultivated. Only one out of every thirty or forty oysters has a pearl.

After doing business in Bangkok, or on a quiet weekend, a side trip to Chiang Mai Province and to the Burmese border, where the "real" trading takes place, was an adventure that combined danger and excitement with tourism. It also exposed me to Burmese rubies, which I could compare with the usual dark red cabochon rubies sold in the jewelry shops of Bangkok and Hong Kong. It is said that the Mogok mines in Burma are exhausted; however, Burma still seems to produce some high-priced rubies and "pigeon blood" rubies. There are also some lovely Burmese royal blue sapphires. One can find some of these top blue sapphires in Thailand as well, with deposits located near Chanthaburi and Kanchanaburi. I have visited both these sites as they are within short trips of Bangkok.

On another visit to Northern India and Kashmir, while on Lake Dal in a small wooden boat, a trader in another boat had a beautiful strand of emerald beads—beads of unusual quality and color for a small dealer. It had been nestled in his pile of silver and handicraft tourist items. Bargaining was expected, but the unexpected occurred when the trader and I began playing catch with the beads from boat to boat across the water. Each time I rejected his price, I would toss them back to him; then he would toss them back to me with a new price and a grin. They were the beginning of what is now an even more interesting multistrand emerald necklace, currently in a private collection. Kashmir also brought me an appreciation of the special sapphires that were once mined near Srinagar. Many of the stones that are sold as Kashmir sapphires today come from other areas such as Burma.

In New Delhi I went to a sari shop in order to buy a sari for my daughter and ended up finding a sapphire bracelet in the owner's quarters that kept me busy in negotiations for the whole time it took my daughter to have the dress designed. Now the bracelet *and* the dress look fine on her. Also, I had the chance to stay in the Maharajah's quarters in a palace that had been converted to a hotel, and to think of the Maharajah's (or Maharani's) jewels that would have been left in those quarters while the Maharani was off on a tiger hunt.

Hong Kong jewelers have long prided themselves on knowing what's in style, but while the glitter was there, the styles were actually lagging. On many occasions while doing business in Hong Kong, I began to teach some of my friendly jewelers how to improve their use of stones and styles to avoid some of the sameness one would see from shop to shop. With their ability to learn quickly, and with the availability of good labor at low cost, it was a chance to "invent" jewelry pieces and make use of the great abundance of stones that were shipped from around the world to this trading port for resetting and resale. The results were usually close to what I designed, which made them unique.

In other cities, big and small, after taking cabs to little jewelry workshops, I was often disappointed because the big and sometimes better stones had been shipped away to the jewelry capitals of the world—with the smaller, lesser stones left behind to be recut or disguised for local tourist pieces. But this made the surprise finds even more interesting. By the same token, in many countries the surprise at finding a customer in a remote area or at a mining site would please the seller.

In Chinese shops it was good to be the first customer, for you would get a better price. The tradition was to start the day as soon as possible with a sale for better luck all day. Being a repeat customer to a friendly merchant also meant a better chance for a good price. Many times, knowing the local customs and beliefs was a help in making myself be at the right place at the right time.

Aboard ship in remote ports, it is not unusual for a local salesman to bring you a handkerchief-tied packet of stones to choose from. A knowledge of the relative value of the stones, as well as an idea of how you want to use them in a setting, helps. In some cases, I have passed up good stones, without realizing their value, that I would later have liked to have had, but these are the small regrets that come with the pleasure.

In countries where goods have more value than money, I found that a pair of Levi's or some American T-shirts could be turned into a good precious or semiprecious guard ring. Once after trading what I had to trade on one South Pacific island, all I had left were some New Zealand airline slippers. I traded these for a local wood carving that later took the interest of the purser on a ship I joined. He traded a piece of pre-Columbian gold jewelry from Ecuador for the wood carving, and I now have a beautiful piece of jewelry in exchange for free airline slippers. Not every trade is that easy, though, or that successful.

AFRICA

In African countries precious stones and their look-alikes can become very confusing. It is always worth a second look before buying or even dismissing a stone. You'll find some of these "copycat" stones in countries like Zambia and Namibia, not just in South Africa and Tanzania. While you would feel perfectly comfortable choosing your stones at a reputable store, you can never assume anything while out in the field. Some common mistaken identities in stones can include aquamarines taken for topazes, tanzanite for sapphires, and spinels for rubies. South African diamond mines, like the Kimberley, the Premier, and the Oranjemund on the west coast, are able to give the amateur an instructive tour. But it still takes years of discerning among a multitude of shades, hues, and nuances of color to achieve connoisseurship in the world of gems.

The Medina in Fez yielded a surprise stone or two, and "trading" was in order. When one is looking for collectibles, it makes *every* new place interesting.

Chilean wine region.

Easter Island.

Thailand.

Boarding in Singapore.

With children Todd, Beatrix, and Trevor at the Kimberley Mine.

Mining site.

Korea.

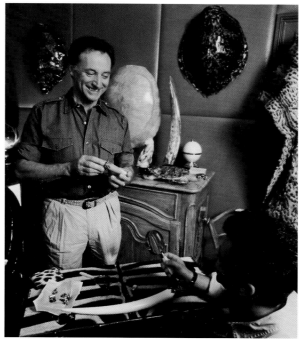

Trading stones.

Brazilian stones.

In various countries of South America the bad political climate at one time or another encouraged people to sell their antiques, including jewelry. And although it was an embarrassment to me, sellers were happy to have you come to their homes or *estancias*, whether in Lima or elsewhere, to pick pieces that one might be interested in buying. After Perón, there were several jewelry stores in Buenos Aires selling fabulous French jewelry rumored to be from the collection of Evita Perón. The jewels were good and the prices were "very negotiable." Once, my mother admired a necklace from this historical collection, returned empty-handed to the United States, and sent me back to retrieve it—at my expense, of course.

In Argentina the rhodochrosite was worth searching for in a good raspberry red. This rhodochrosite was said to have formed as stalagmites in the Incan mines.

In Colombia I did business in Bogotá, Cartagena, and Cali at a time when street shopping or city travel was not as treacherous as it may be now, but it still had its risks. Being streetwise, I would find emeralds—some of which I hoped came from the great Colombian emerald mines such as Muzo or Chivor and at streetwise prices. With so many emeralds in Colombia moving through backdoor markets, it was worth a try. After many years spotting good green stones, I felt happy with the results.

On the way to one shop in Cartagena, my shipmates were introduced to a new trick in street shopping. There were small gangs of young thieves who would sneak up behind you and cut your belt with a sharp knife. While you were pulling up your pants, there went your watch, your camera, your bags, and your jewelry—and sometimes your pride. The gangs of boys had many such tricks up their sleeves for tourists. It was their own way of collecting gems.

I found some emeralds in Brazil and India, but they were disappointing in comparison with Colombian stones. I also searched for lapis lazuli in Chile and Peru—different from the gem lapis found in Afghanistan but occasionally in an Afghan blue and sometimes attractively carved for a tabletop ornament. When my travels took me to mining towns in Chile such as Rancagua, I looked in my spare time for Chilean stones. In Peru an occasional necklace said to come from an Inca grave would remind me of a French jewelry design.

Searching for the best dark rubellite in Rio or São Paulo was a challenge, no small part of which was driving to the stores in a Rio cab. For, to me, a good rubellite (which ranges in color from a pale rose-red to deep ruby-red) was as pretty as a ruby, but at only a fraction of the cost. For instance, and without trying to oversimplify a complicated grading system for stones, one might find a 5- to 8-carat ruby at around $15,000 per carat, while a rubellite of approximately the same size and quality range would cost you only about $300 per carat.

A search for stones in Ipanema is good adventure too. The view of the beach can be surpassed only by the glitter of the jewelry stores.

Jewelry trips may sound like pleasure, but in many cases there are dangers connected with them because you're shopping in countries with political upheaval, poverty, and a degree of lawlessness. All of which add to the intrigue, excitement, and adrenaline level. Leaving a shop in Buenos Aires with an armed guard—not because of the jewelry but because you're making a business call to the American ambassador—gives one more to remember.

ITALY

During the high period of Italian jewelry from Florence, it was interesting to visit the workshops that supplied not only the Ponte Vecchio but the jewelers of Rome and Milan, and to deal directly with the jewelry workers and designers, to get pieces from the source.

Visiting the Costa Smeralda in Sardinia in season has given me a glimpse of what it may have been like in Biarritz and Monte Carlo in an earlier day. All of the jewelers' wares are available for sale when you step off your yacht. If you need something for a party that night, you might borrow a piece and return it the next day. Of course, you may decide to purchase it, which the jewelers hope for, and that is what usually happens. The "name" jewelers are there in season, as they are in St. Moritz and now in other resorts, including Aspen.

THE UNITED STATES

My journeys have also included various destinations in the United States, although my search there has centered more on minerals than on gems. Mineral collectors, however, will tell tales of finding rubies in Montana and North Carolina, as well as sapphires in Montana, although there has been no sapphire mining there since the 1920s. Rocks with emeralds can come from Connecticut, Maine, or North Carolina, but generally the semiprecious stones are more likely to be found in U.S. mineral shops.

Jewelry has many lives, and often the stones themselves seem to have lives of their own. With the help of the most extraordinary jewelry from the great designers and jewelry firms, I hope to fascinate and enchant the reader.

—John Traina

Emerald-and-diamond ring; six bees hold the center 7.62-carat emerald. Designed by Jean Schlumberger
for Tiffany & Co. (Courtesy Tiffany & Co., San Francisco)
Andrew Edgar

EXTRAORDINARY JEWELS

Introduction

$\mathcal{P}$recious stones have exercised a fascination from the beginning of time. They have been looked upon as talismans to help resist evil, preserve health, and cure disease. They were also thought to have supernatural powers to fend off ghosts. Some jewels have been wrapped for centuries in a cloak of mystery or lost from sight and found again. Gems have been a reason for high crimes, or objects of love, desire, and even veneration. Beautiful stones have engendered corruption, deceit, avarice, and obsession. They have been sought after with intensity and determination, endlessly traded, and frequently plundered. However, the unvarying trait that most of them share is that they exude an aura of power and wealth and are wonderful to own and wear. Today, as in the past, they are still regarded as an excellent, portable investment.

The first known gemstones included emeralds, amethysts, garnets, turquoise, and rock crystal. Other highly prized adornments—organic materials and thus not technically gemstones—were pearls, coral, and amber. But for many centuries the precious stones considered most precious have been diamonds, rubies, sapphires, emeralds, and (still) pearls. Of all these, it is diamonds that hold center stage in terms of glamour and excitement.

According to the book *Tiffany Taste*—an informal history of the great jewelry house—experts have estimated that by the 1880s a small number of Americans owned over a billion dollars' worth of diamonds. This would have been more than all the crowned heads of Europe—with the exception of Queen Victoria—together. Tiffany's sales of the time were more than $6 million a year for diamonds, and the same amount or more for pearls, emeralds, rubies, and sapphires. When translated into modern money, the figure is staggering. As an example, a 9-carat diamond classed as white and flawless could be bought for $2,000 in those days. Near the end of the twentieth century, a gem like that would cost $600,000 to $700,000.

DIAMONDS

Diamonds are the stones by which the world is most likely to measure success in wealth and material achievement. And it is primarily through the acquisition, design, and sale of diamonds that jewelers become distinguished.

Diamond butterfly brooch from the mid-nineteenth century containing six antique cushion-cut diamonds and numerous old-mine diamonds.
Copyright © 1988 Sotheby's, Inc.

Westminster tiara, circa 1930, has scroll and crescent motifs of old-mine, baguette, marquise-shaped, and pear-shaped diamonds.
Two detachable pear-shaped clusters can be worn either as a pair of clips or attached to a bangle.
Copyright © 1988 Sotheby's, Inc.

Diamonds were first discovered in India—some say as far back as 400 B.C.—and many fabled stones were mined there. Then, in the eighteenth century, diamonds were discovered in Brazil. In the mid-nineteenth century a stone identified as a diamond was found in South Africa, and the rush was on. Africa today is the primary source for gem-quality diamonds, although they have also been mined in quantity in Siberia and Australia.

Finding and processing the gem are a labor-intensive industry. An enormous amount of diamond-bearing rock must be mined and processed to produce a 1-carat diamond. And of the diamonds found, only about 20 percent are of gem quality.

"If a diamond possesses perfect qualities, it is to be desired above all other jewels." So an Indian connoisseur of the Gupta period was said to have remarked well over a thousand years ago. This desirability may have been found in the diamond's "magic ability" to break white light into all the colors of the spectrum. This prismatic function must have seemed supernatural indeed.

In India the possession of diamonds was dictated by caste—only Brahmins would have been allowed to own pure, colorless diamonds. Property owners, the next level down, could possess diamonds tinted with a hint of yellow. Quite yellowish stones were for merchants and traders.

In every age, cultures have ascribed to diamonds romantic, practical, and erroneous attributes. It is said that the Greeks saw diamonds as fragments of stars that had fallen to earth. The Romans thought diamonds so hard they could break iron. But the Chinese treasured diamonds for their utilitarian engraving ability. Today diamonds are the stones used in engagement rings to pledge eternal love—possibly because they are so hard as to be virtually indestructible.

The Diamond Information Center, headquartered in New York City, is the consumer information bureau for the diamond jewelry industry in the United States. It offers information on fashion trends, as well as telling consumers what they should look for when purchasing a stone. The Center is headquartered within N W Ayer, the marketing communications company that has represented De Beers in the United States since 1938.

WHITE DIAMONDS

The Koh-i-Noor, a famous 186-carat diamond associated with the British royal family, was presented to Queen Victoria in 1850 by the East India Company and put on public display the following year. But the gem failed to fulfill general expectations. Consequently, the Koh-i-Noor (Mountain of Light) was recut for brilliance: the 108.93-carat stone that resulted was a dazzler. Superstition had it that only a female ruler could wear the jewel. After Victoria, the diamond was set into the crowns of three queens consort in succession: Alexandra, Mary, and finally Elizabeth (the Queen Mother). In this setting it is displayed among the British crown jewels in the Tower of London.

The Cullinan is the largest gem-quality diamond rock ever found. The stone, discovered in 1905 at the Premier mine in the Transvaal, was so enormous—3,106 carats (about 1.3 pounds)—that even cutting it into 105 stones, plus 9 more carats of polished bits, still yielded the first- and second-largest diamonds in the world. The Cullinan I, also known as the Great Star of Africa, is a pear-shape weighing 530 carats, white and flawless. It is set in the royal Scepter but can be removed to be worn as a pendant. The Cullinan II, the Lesser Star of Africa, is a cushion-shaped diamond weighing 317 carats that sits at the front of the imperial crown, just under the Black Prince's spinel ruby.

When the rough stone was presented to Edward VII on his sixty-sixth birthday in 1907, the Amsterdam firm of I. J. Asscher was called on to cut it. Joseph Asscher prepared the gem and finally, on a day in February 1908, he placed the cleaving blade on the jewel and tapped with a weighty rod. The blade broke; the stone remained intact. But the second tap was triumphant. The stone cleaved in two—and Asscher fell down in a dead faint.

The next two Cullinan diamonds down in size were set in Queen Mary's crown, but are removable and can be worn combined as a single brooch of 158 carats. These are now the private property of Queen Elizabeth. Almost all the rest of the Cullinan "chips"—the nine major stones weighing from 94.5 down to 4.4 carats—also belong to the Queen.

The Taylor-Burton diamond won a place in history by playing a part in one of the greatest love stories of our time. The 69.42-carat pear-shaped gem had been cut from a 241-carat rough stone by Harry Winston and sold in 1967 to Harriet Annenberg Ames, sister of Walter Annenberg. Two years later it was put up for auction in New York. The understanding was that it would be named after its purchaser, who, it was believed, would be a certain world-famous film star. However, Cartier bought it, for $1,050,000. Four days later it was sold for $1,100,000 to Richard Burton, who purchased it as a gift for Elizabeth Taylor. The jewel was immediately named Taylor-Burton, and Cartier wrung some additional publicity out of the sale by displaying the jewel in Chicago and New York. Ten years later Elizabeth Taylor had become Mrs. John Warner and the romantic gem was resold to a jeweler in New York.

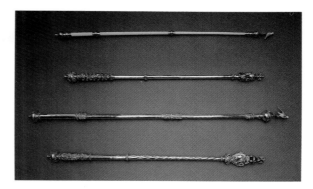

LEFT, *Queen Elizabeth the Queen Mother's crown.*
British Crown copyright. Reproduced with the permission of the Controller of Her
Britannic Majesty's Stationery Office.

RIGHT TOP, *composite of scepters and rods.*
British Crown copyright. Reproduced with the permission of the Controller of Her Britannic Majesty's Stationery Office.

RIGHT BOTTOM, *sovereign's Orb and Scepter.*
British Crown copyright. Reproduced with the permission of the Controller of Her Britannic Majesty's Stationery Office.

The Orlov diamond is a stone associated with unrequited passion—and unachieved power. The 189.60-carat gem is one of several speculated to be the stone cut from the Great Mogul diamond of Shah Jahan. That diamond disappeared in 1739, possibly as part of the plunder of Delhi by the Persian Nadir Shah. Prince Orlov bought the stone in Amsterdam in 1775 and presented it to Catherine the Great, with whom he had fallen out of favor both romantically and politically. The Empress of Russia, who was said to have loved jewels so well she had her own gem-cutting operation in the Urals, accepted the gift—but not the discarded lover. The Orlov diamond was mounted above the double eagle in the imperial scepter and is now housed in the Diamond Fund of the Kremlin.

The Centenary is a relatively recent entry into the list of giant diamonds. In its rough state, the Centenary emerged in 1988 from the Premier mine in South Africa weighing 599 carats. This was the same mine in which the Cullinan had been found. It took three years to cut and polish the remarkable Centenary, but it ended up as a 273-carat gem, one of the largest flawless D-color diamonds in the world.

Colored diamonds are very rare. About 1 in 100,000 diamonds has the deep natural color necessary to qualify as a fine fancy-colored diamond. Among these, the rarest is the intensely red diamond, followed closely by the pure green. Blue diamonds are another rarity, but rank in desirability below red and green. Pink diamonds are also rare, but less so than reds or pure greens. The yellow can range from a brown-tinged champagne color through lemon yellow to an orange-yellow known as jonquil.

Fancy-colored diamonds have shown a marked increase in price over the last decade or so. One jewelry firm executive suggested that it is because of their rarity they are sought by the affluent buyer looking for something no one else has. Of course, buyers are also attracted by the sheer beauty of the colors. And finally, they represent a store of wealth. It is not surprising that fancy-colored diamonds—which is how they are referred to in the trade—have been setting record prices.

A complete array of every recognized color in diamonds can be seen in the Gumuchian Collection in the Morgan Memorial Hall of Gems at the American Museum of Natural History in New York City. The stones are a sampler of the diamond spectrum, but a few famous stones should also be mentioned.

The Great Table was a magnificent pink stone that, when cut, yielded two fabulous pink diamonds. One is the Darya-i-Nur (Sea of Light), an estimated 185 carats, which may be the finest pink diamond in the world; the other, at 60 carats, is the Nur-al-Ain (Light of the Eye). When Delhi was overrun by the Persians in 1739, the Persian Shah stole the Mogul treasure, including the Great Table (the name refers to its flat cut), and those gems became the basis of the royal Iranian treasury of jewels.

The Golconda d'Or is one of the last big diamonds taken from the fabled mines in Golconda, India. The beautiful yellow stone was another treasure of the Mogul emperors of India that was plundered by the Persians. The 95.4-carat gem was fashioned from a 130-carat uncut jewel in the 1950s and is believed to be the largest golden emerald-cut diamond in the world. (The yellow diamond considered to be the largest and finest in existence is the Tiffany, held by the store after which it was named.) The Golconda d'Or was given to the Sultan of Turkey early in the nineteenth century, then went into a private collection. In 1960 it was acquired by an Australian jeweler, Dunklings, was stolen sometime after 1978, and has not yet been recovered (see "Jewel Thefts").

The Hope diamond is the stone to which more stories have been attached than any other gem. Besides being a large pure stone of extraordinary color—a very deep blue—its fabled status derives from its supposed curse. It was thought that anyone who owned it was risking a terrible and mysterious fate. However, its place among the anecdotes of gemological history has been fixed primarily by only one person, its last private owner, the wealthy and eccentric Evalyn Walsh McLean.

A very large and rare sapphire-blue diamond was mined in the vicinity of Golconda, India, and eventually obtained by the much-traveled French merchant Jean-Baptiste Tavernier, who sold it to Louis XIV of France in 1669. To bring out its brilliance, it was cut about four years later to a 69-carat heart-shaped stone (and cut at a later date to its present cushion shape). The gem was worn by the Sun King of Versailles in a variety of ways.

LEFT, *yellow South African heart-shaped diamond ring,*
held in a private collection.
Fred Lyon

RIGHT, *extremely rare fancy green diamond pendant containing one*
emerald-cut green diamond weighing 8.19 carats, partially enveloped by
marquise-shaped diamonds. Because of its color and large size, this stone is
considered among the most notable diamonds in the world.
Copyright © 1983 Sotheby's, Inc.

The Blue Diamond of the Crown, as it was called, was inherited by his great-grandson and successor, Louis XV, who had it set in an ornament known as the Golden Fleece. As Louis XIV reigned comfortably for much of the seventeenth century and part of the eighteenth, and Louis XV also had a splendid court and a long reign, the curse seems not yet to have been in effect. And one could hardly blame a diamond for the French Revolution and the fall of the next royal inheritor, Louis XVI. (Although the famous scandal of the diamond necklace [see "Jewel Thefts"] argues otherwise.)

In 1792 the French crown jewels were stolen from the Garde-Meuble and disappeared. The diamond may have gone to the Spanish court; there is a 1799 painting by Goya of the royal family showing Queen María Luisa wearing a large blue stone. In any case, a beautiful dark blue diamond showed up in London in the first quarter of the nineteenth century. Supposedly it had come via Amsterdam (there it was probably recut to its present shape and size of 45.52 carats). There is also a lurid element: legend has the cutter's son stealing the diamond and committing suicide, and the diamond cutter dying of grief. However, no records survive of the persons in this tale.

What is known is that the diamond was purchased in London in 1830 or somewhat before. Its new owner, a member of a banking family and a collector of fancy-colored diamonds, was Henry Philip Hope. It was he who gave its present name to the gem, which passed down through succeeding Hope heirs until it finally reached the hands of Lord Henry Francis Hope, who was something of a wastrel. Lord Hope wanted to sell the diamond to pay gambling debts. A long period of court litigation between him and other family members followed; he was finally given permission to sell the jewel in 1901.

The curse seems to have been quiescent during the Hope family's ownership, but rumors spring up again in the interval between one long-term owner and the next. The tales include suicide, murder, and fatal accidents, none ever substantiated.

Early in the century the jewel may for a while have been in the collection of the Sultan of Turkey. In 1909 a gem dealer named Rosenau may have bought the jewel, which was next sold to Pierre Cartier of the famous Paris house. There is speculation that it was Pierre Cartier who invented the story of the curse.

Evalyn Walsh McLean, the prominent Washington hostess who was soon to buy it, was not interested in the diamond when she first saw it, in 1910; but she told Cartier that objects which brought misfortune to others had just the opposite effect on her. Pierre Cartier persevered. Later that year, having had the diamond reset in a splendid necklace, he visited Mrs. McLean and urged her to keep the stone over a weekend. Proximity did the trick; the sale was made.

As a kind of insurance, she took the diamond to a priest to have it blessed, then put it on and scarcely ever took it off. It is said that at one point when she was to have surgery, the doctor had to implore her to remove it. Outrageously flamboyant, she would often wear all her famous jewels at the same time, especially when she was entertaining, which she did a great deal. Once she was asked why she wore all her dazzling jewelry at once; she answered, "Then I know where it is." At the apparently rare moments when the Hope was not around her neck, it was stored in the back of a tabletop radio. It has been said that Mrs. McLean hung it around the neck of her Great Dane, Mike, and gave it to her son, Jock, to teethe on.

Curiously, as the only owner who publicly scoffed at the stone's ostensible powers, she did experience great misfortune. Mrs. McLean's marriage to a heavy-drinking husband ended in divorce; he died in a mental institution. A brother of hers died untimely, and shortly after that her eldest son, only nine years old, was run over and killed. The final blow was the death of her only daughter, who took an overdose of pills in 1946, when she was twenty-five. This last death seemed to be more than Mrs. McLean could bear. She herself died of pneumonia a year later, when she was sixty. Coincidentally, her granddaughter Evalyn McLean also died at the age of twenty-five, in 1967.

Mrs. McLean's jewelry was bequeathed to her grandchildren, but the court granted them a petition to sell the collection to pay estate debts. In 1949 the jeweler Harry Winston bought all Mrs. McLean's jewels. He displayed the Hope to raise money for charity and in 1958 gave the famous blue diamond—touted in lurid headlines for its "Legacy of Doom"—to the Smithsonian Institution, where it immediately increased attendance. Thus the curse, if there was one, seems to have been broken.

RUBIES

Rubies of great size, perfection, and intense color are the rarest of all precious gems. A perfect ruby of above 4 carats begins to be very rare. The world's premier source for rubies is in a mining area called the Mogok Stone Tract in upper Burma. The mines fell into the hands of the King of Burma at the end of the sixteenth century, but it was not until after the British took control of the country in 1886 that the Mogok mines reached their full potential, soon after yielding their famous rubies of intense crimson called pigeon's

This important diamond-and-ruby sautoir centers around a cabochon ruby weighing approximately 16 carats, with slightly graduated ruby beads and diamond pavé links suspending a ruby bead tassel. Signed by M. Gérard.
Christie's New York

blood. A recent example in the public eye: a 15.97-carat cushion-cut Mogok ruby, exceptionally free of flaws and in the prized deep red color, purchased by the jeweler Laurence Graff.

The largest gem ruby yet found is a Burmese stone of 400 carats. Another ruby phenomenon with Burmese origins is a belt buckle (among the former Iranian crown jewels) made up of eighty-four cabochon rubies, some up to 11 carats in size.

In the late 1980s rubies—as well as sapphires of very fine quality—were discovered in Vietnam, northwest of Hanoi. Both the Luc Yen and Quy Chau mining regions are yielding stones that in many cases compete head-to-head with their Burmese counterparts. The stones are similar in color and internal characteristics. As a result, rubies from Vietnam are occasionally confused with, and even sold as, Burmese stones from Mogok. Despite attempts at government control, the new mines are experiencing what mining regions the world over have long accepted as a way of life: smuggling. Smugglers bring their uncut stones to large cities, where the buyer must beware. Synthetic rubies mixed among genuine stones can also pose a risk.

Although these fabulous stones from Vietnam have not yet made a major impact on international gem markets, prominent jewelry firms are certainly aware of them and have been sending their representatives to the country. This new source will undoubtedly prove significant in the future gem trade.

Some rubies, like sapphires, show a rayed formation called a star. Two major star rubies in public collections are the Reeves (138.7 carats) at the Smithsonian Institution, and the De Long (100 carats) at the American Museum of Natural History.

In the last century it was discovered that some "rubies" are not rubies at all but spinels, a similar-looking gem. Two famous historical rubies now listed as spinel rubies are the Black Prince's ruby, set in the British Imperial State Crown, and the Timur ruby, set in a necklace among the British crown jewels.

SAPPHIRES

Sapphires, gems much favored by the British royal family, are actually sister stones to rubies. Both are varieties of the same very hard mineral, corundum. But sapphires are not as rare as rubies; the element that primarily colors rubies red (chromium) is scarcer in nature than iron, the pigmentation element that makes sapphires blue.

Not that all sapphires are blue. The gem can be found in nature in a variety of colors, from colorless to green, yellow, orange, pink, purple, and black. But *only* the blue gem is simply called sapphire, and it is considered the most valuable. Large sapphires of very fine quality and beautiful color are relatively unusual, although as a rule gem-quality sapphires are found in larger sizes than rubies.

The color of choice in blue sapphires is the true cornflower blue—slightly pale with a touch of violet and a kind of velvety sheen. Kashmir in India was the great source for these gems, but those deposits have not been actively worked for years. In addition, the mines lie high in the Himalayas and are covered with snow and ice over most of the year.

EMERALDS

Second only to rubies, emeralds were greatly esteemed in antiquity, and have been considered more valuable than comparable diamonds. They were treasured in early Egypt and cherished in ancient Greece and Rome; in pre-Columbian Mexico and Peru, they were intricately and skillfully cut and carved. The emerald cut, a type of step cut in which the four corners of the "steps" are faceted to create an octagonal shape, was developed because the brittle emerald is so sensitive to knocks.

Emeralds, valued for their deep green color, are the most precious members of the beryl family, which includes aquamarines and green beryls.

The most important emerald deposits are in Colombia, especially the Muzo mine, which is said to produce emeralds by which all others are judged. The mine goes well back into history. It was worked by the Incas, abandoned, and then rediscovered in the seventeenth century. Other sites in Colombia that yield high-quality gems are the Chivor mine and the Gachala deposit. Although Colombia has tried to maintain controls over the sale of emeralds, most of the mined stones are smuggled out.

The Habach Valley area of Austria does not produce first-grade stones but is important historically as a site mined by the Romans. Today emeralds are also found in Brazil, Zambia, Zimbabwe, and Pakistan.

The Topkapi Museum in Istanbul, the Smithsonian Institution in Washington, D.C., and the American Museum of Natural History in New York all have displays of notable cut and polished emeralds, as well as uncut crystals. In the Kunsthistorisches Museum in Vienna there is an extraordinary vase carved out of a single 2,681-carat emerald crystal. And there is in a private collection a 45-carat emerald, called the Atahuallpa, that is part of the Crown of the Andes, a stunning gold headpiece set with 453 emeralds totaling 1,521 carats.

OPPOSITE, *French Art Deco carved emerald–and–diamond demi-parure showing a fringe necklace of pavé-set baguette, trapeze, round, and bullet-cut diamonds suspending fluted emerald drops. The two detachable chandelier clusters may be added at the back of the necklace. Signed by Ostertag, France. Christie's New York*

ABOVE, *20.82-carat emerald-cut emerald ring, its two rows of thirty-six round diamonds (set in platinum) creating an octagonal shape.* Copyright © 1983 Sotheby's Inc.

Until the early years of this century, natural, or "Oriental," pearls were more costly than diamonds and were considered the most valuable of all jewels. That fact may be hard to take in, given the broad availability of cultured pearls today.

Strings of pearls roped over the bosom and down to the waist were the style before the turn of the century. Women were said to favor pearls because they found them more becoming than colored stones. Strands could cost $300,000 or more in 1900 dollars. If one were truly rich, three sets worn simultaneously were practically de rigueur.

Pearls are formed inside the shells of mollusks, most notably oysters. (Freshwater pearls are found in mussels.) The animal reacts to an irritant, such as a grain of sand, by coating it with concentric layers of a translucent substance called nacre. A pearl's lustrous iridescent glow is the result of the refraction of light through these layers. The best natural pearls came from the Persian Gulf, which has been fished for two thousand years. They were also obtained from the South Seas.

The natural pearl has been supplanted in the gem markets by the cultured pearl, also a natural product, albeit one formed with a little help from the hand of man. They are particularly associated with Japan, where the culturing process was perfected (see "Mikimoto" under "Extraordinary Jewelers A–Z").

Large cultured pearls from the South Seas—generally over 10 millimeters in diameter—are particularly sought-after today. They are obtained from culturing operations in Burma, Australia, and Tahiti, habitat of the larger oysters. Round South Sea pearls, as well as off-shape "baroque" pearls, are extremely costly, comparable to those used to create the fabulous natural pearl necklaces of bygone eras. In 1990 a strand of enormous cultured pearls sold for $2.2 million at auction.

Pearls range in color from white and cream to rose, yellow, and gold. Black cultured pearls, particularly associated with Tahiti, are found in a range of shades from pale gray to gunmetal. Pearls also range greatly in size, from extremely small "dust" pearls to tiny seed pearls (under 3 millimeters) to rice-shaped pearls associated with Japan's Lake Biwa. A "Rice Krispie" pearl of lesser quality has become a rather common export of China. The largest pearl found to date, 450 carats, is in the South Kensington Geological Museum in London.

La Peregrina, the famed pear-shaped pearl owned by Elizabeth Taylor, was once part of the Spanish crown jewels. The actress acquired it for $37,000 from Sotheby's in 1969 and had it mounted by Cartier in a pearl-and-diamond choker.

TOP, *tiara with pearls adorns Princess Diana.*
Tim Graham/SYGMA

BOTTOM, *pearls.*
Copyright © David Doubilet

Jewels in the Smithsonian Collection

*O*ne of the best places to see extraordinary jewels is in the gem collection at the Smithsonian's National Museum of Natural History in Washington, D.C., where there is a dazzling display of polished stones, specimen rocks, and varied minerals. As a drawing card, the star of the collection is undoubtedly the fabled Hope diamond, already discussed. Since 1958, when Harry Winston sent his headline-making donation to the Smithsonian in an ordinary package wrapped in brown paper, many other jewels have been contributed for display.

The Hooker emerald, a 1977 gift from Janet Annenberg Hooker, was believed to have adorned the belt buckle of a Turkish sultan in the late nineteenth century. The beautifully hued 75-carat gem, now a brooch surrounded by diamonds, was acquired by Tiffany & Co. before World War I. Mrs. Hooker bought it at a "white elephant sale" at the elegant emporium in 1955—one of only two such in the company's history.

The Logan sapphire, one of the largest blue sapphires in the world (at 423 carats it is the size of a goose egg), was given to the museum in 1960 by Rebecca Guggenheim Logan. Its provenance is unclear, but Mrs. Logan had said it once belonged to a maharajah. The brilliant deep blue stone is set as a brooch surrounded by twenty clear diamonds.

The Thompson diamonds came to the gem collection in 1990 from Libby Moody Thompson. They were cut from a 264-carat stone of an unprepossessing brown tone, but Harry Winston spotted its potential when he saw the rough gem in Antwerp. What emerged were three remarkable cognac-colored pear-shapes weighing a total of 73 carats. They were made into a brooch with matching earrings.

The Smithsonian has some famous royal jewelry among its gems, including the adornments of two monarchs of France, Empress Marie Louise and Queen Marie Antoinette.

LEFT, *the Logan sapphire.*
Smithsonian Institution Photo No. 77-10626

MIDDLE, *the Hooker emerald.*
Smithsonian Institution Photo No. 77-14194

RIGHT, *the Hope diamond.*
Smithsonian Institution Photo No. 78-8853

LEFT, *the Napoleon necklace.*
Smithsonian Institution Photo No. 78-10489

MIDDLE ABOVE, *the Marie Louise diadem.*
Smithsonian Institution Photo No. 77-12984

MIDDLE BELOW, *the Marie Antoinette earrings.*
Smithsonian Institution Photo No. 85-14950

RIGHT, *the Thompson diamonds.*
(Courtesy Smithsonian Institution, National Museum of Natural History)
Chip Clark

The Napoleon necklace, given by the first Emperor of France to his Empress, Marie Louise, is considered by some to be the finest piece of Napoleonic jewelry in this country. Given on the occasion of the birth of their son in 1811, the dazzling necklace went to the royal house of Austria after Marie Louise's death in 1847 and was passed down through the Hapsburgs. The jewel, comprising forty-seven diamonds, has a light, floating look despite its 275 carats. It was acquired in 1960 by Harry Winston, who sold it to Marjorie Merriweather Post, a benefactor of the museum.

The Marie Louise diadem, according to an entry in a Louvre catalogue, was a wedding gift from Napoleon to his bride in 1810. The piece was part of a parure consisting of the tiara, a necklace, earrings, a buckle, and a comb all made by the Paris firm Nitot et Fils. The silver diadem was set with seventy-nine emeralds and about a thousand brilliants, or antique-cut diamonds. It, too, became part of the Hapsburgs' collection on the Empress's death. Subsequent to its pur-

chase by Van Cleef & Arpels in 1952, the emeralds were replaced with fine Persian turquoises. The jewel is another of Marjorie Merriweather Post's bequests.

The Marie Antoinette earrings may or may not have belonged to that unfortunate French Queen. But their opulent appearance makes them seem fit for a royal personage. Early in his reign Louis XVI gave his Queen earrings with pear-shaped diamonds pendant from a cluster of diamonds. Supposedly she was so fond of the jewels that she wore them constantly and took them with her when the royal family attempted to flee France in 1791. When the family was stopped, the earrings were said to have been confiscated. Other reports have the earrings lost in the looting of the French crown jewels in 1792. In any case, at least four pairs of Marie Antoinette earrings were mentioned in records of European gem sales during the nineteenth century. This particular pair ended up in the possession of Prince Felix Youssoupov, who sold them to Pierre Cartier, from whom Marjorie Merriweather Post bought them in 1928.

EXTRAORDINARY JEWELERS A-Z

*I*n this section I discuss some of the great names in jewelry and look at what they themselves see as their best work. By using quotes and opinions, as well as some lively anecdotes, I believe I have made the book more revealing. I have devoted less discussion to designers and emporiums no longer in business because I wanted to consider great jewels from the point of view of those working (or at least available) today. The designers featured in this book are, for the most part, those of whom the public has been made aware through jewelry sales, but I also discuss some of those lesser-known designers of which only a select clientele may now be aware.

The photographs used represent the work of photographers Fred Lyon and Andrew Edgar as well as the cream of what was available to reproduce, and the best of the archives.

Gold, platinum, peridot, and diamond "Fantasy Necklace" designed by Salvador Dali, made by Charles Valliant, circa 1965.
The upper portion is a gold choker necklace composed of links resembling bricks and decorated with three lion's-head masks, their eyes set with six small round emeralds.
Jets of water formed of baguette diamonds stream from their mouths and terminate in a pool of numerous peridots, studded with round diamonds.
The whole set includes 175 baguette diamonds weighing approximately 20.00 carats, 100 round diamonds weighing approximately 15.00 carats,
and 184 emerald-cut, pear-shaped, cushion-shaped, and round peridots; the peridot section is detachable.
*   Also shown is a gold, peridot, and diamond ring designed by Salvador Dali, made by Charles Valliant. The cushion-shaped peridot is mounted in a textured gold*
prong, decorated at the sides with lion's-head masks set with three cabochon-emerald eyes and eighteen baguette diamonds.

ASPREY

*A*sprey was established in 1781 by William Asprey, a descendant of a Huguenot family that had escaped from France to England. Like many of the French Protestants who fled persecution under Louis XIV, William's forebears were skilled craftsmen—metalsmiths, leatherworkers, watchmakers. By the middle of the nineteenth century the growing company acquired a larger building and expanded into another street. The shop, which was still being enlarged in the 1930s, is situated on New Bond Street in the heart of London.

During the nineteenth century Asprey became known for making handsomely appointed dressing cases with sterling silver fittings, soon changing the construction to fine leather instead of the more cumbersome wood. In 1859 Asprey bought out a company in Holborn that had been warranted as a traveling-case maker to Queen Victoria, and had the benefit not only of the royal appointment but of acquiring skilled craftsmen as well. In the famous Crystal Palace exhibition of 1851, Asprey had managed only an honorable mention; but at the International Exhibition in 1862, it received its own warrant from the Queen—and won a gold medal for the high quality of its dressing cases.

In the twentieth century Asprey has become known for its range of jewelry, with luxurious creations at the top of the line. Today the company has royal warrants of appointment as goldsmiths, silversmiths, and jewelers to the Queen, the Queen Mother, and the Prince of Wales. It supplies a good deal of the royal jewelry, but not always directly. As Asprey is particularly favored by Arab monarchs and other Eastern rulers, it has been commissioned to fashion gifts for the Queen and other members of the British royal family. These presents of jewelry from one monarch or royal heir to another have with some frequency involved the setting of striking sapphires. The Crown Prince of Saudi Arabia sent as his state wedding present to Diana, Princess of Wales, a magnificent suite of sapphire-and-diamond jewelry made by Asprey. In 1986 the Princess received another fabulous Asprey suite of sapphires and diamonds when she visited the Sultan of Oman. Perhaps the royal family holds the sapphire in such special esteem because it was a handsome sapphire that centered the crown worn by the young Queen Victoria for her coronation.

Asprey takes pride in its services, both that of the retail staff and that of the well-trained and often ingenious artisans in its own workshop at the top of the New Bond Street building. Craftsmen use techniques that have been passed down through generations. They can provide an excellence seldom seen in large-

South Sea Keshi pearls, Burmese rubies, and brilliant-cut diamonds comprise this Asprey pearl bib necklace.
Asprey, New York

This magnificent Asprey necklace of diamonds and a cabochon ruby can convert to a tiara.
Also, the detachable central ruby-and-diamond motif can be worn as a brooch or pendant.
Asprey of Bond Street, London

scale production, enabling them to provide special attention to their customers' requirements. Some requests result in good merchandise ideas.

An American who wanted to be able to brush his teeth after business lunches was accommodated with a 9-karat-gold collapsible toothbrush that telescoped down to the size of a pillbox. Asprey introduced dozens into its stock and sold them all out.

To satisfy another customer, the workshop fashioned a triple-decker egg-and-bacon sandwich—an assignment that must have tested the imagination and skills of the redoubtable Asprey staff. But they rose to the occasion. It seems that there was a Texas millionaire whose favorite lunch was a three-layered sandwich of eggs, with a twist of bacon on top. While doing business in Switzerland, he complained that he could not find a local restaurant that could make a decent high-rise sandwich. The Swiss company with which he was doing business quietly contacted Asprey. Just before the Texan was to depart for home, he received a perfect triple-decker sandwich with eggs and a twist of bacon—in silver gilt. Asprey's craftsmen had actually toasted three slices of bread in the workshop, fried the eggs, and cooked and crisped the bacon. Then they assembled the ingredients into a sandwich, made a mold, and cast it. The silver-gilt sandwich now rests on the Texas millionaire's desk.

Another request came from a maharajah who wanted to make a spousal gift of an emerald-and-diamond bracelet. A sketch was approved and the bracelet was created. The maharajah was so delighted with it that he ordered seven; it turned out he had seven wives.

Asprey has always supplied made-to-order pieces for its clientele, although not generally silver sandwiches or proliferated bracelets. The company has copied family heirlooms in gold or silver and created gem-studded art and decorative pieces.

Asprey continues to make such ornamental objects as swords, daggers, regalia, and badges of honor for foreign governments, oil sheiks, and kings, in addition to supplying the royalty and aristocracy of various countries with silver, glass, china, clocks, and furniture. As far back as 1815 it advertised "articles of exclusive design and high quality, whether for personal adornment or personal accompaniment and to endow with richness and beauty the tables and homes of people of refinement and discernment."

But in spite of its many areas of competence, Asprey is most famous for its jewelry. It will still prepare unique designs on special order, and is recognized for its high standards. The Asprey guarantee is taken seriously.

The company has held royal appointments to every reigning British sovereign since Queen Victoria. Asprey's customer lists have included the British royal family, heads of state, American millionaires such as J. P. Morgan, and maharajahs, including the maharajahs of Patiala and Cooch Behar, as well as the Gaekwar of Baroda and the Sultan of Lahore. Tiaras that rested on many of these heads were made by Asprey, which today continues the tradition.

LEFT, *white-, yellow-, and rose-gold heron brooch set with a pear-shaped aquamarine and pavé diamonds. (Courtesy Asprey, New York)*
Andrew Edgar

RIGHT, *rhino brooch set with pavé diamonds and ruby eyes. (Courtesy Asprey, New York)*
Andrew Edgar

BELPERRON

*S*uzanne Belperron's jewelry was boldly conceived. It had the chic of understatement and the cool enticement of something new. Her work adorned the knowing and the haute monde, from Colette to that indefatigable collector of beautiful and expensive jewelry, the Duchess of Windsor.

Her list of clients included not only women but their admirers and husbands as well. Among those men with a taste for exclusive jewelry: Frank Sinatra, Charlie Chaplin, Gary Cooper, Clark Gable, and the Duke of Windsor.

Belperron custom-designed pieces for her clients as if she were fitting gowns, spending time with them to see what they should wear, arguing that they would not buy clothes off the rack—then why jewels? She admired the French couture designers, particularly Balenciaga, and her jewelry has a quality related to the French fashion of the 1930s.

She rarely made more than one of any piece. Her pride in what she could do was such that she refused to sign her work, saying that her designs should be instantly recognizable. Collecting old Belperron jewelry thus becomes a little risky because of imitators.

She avoided using stones that were simply commercially available, jeweler Christopher Walling recalls, and instead used chalcedony, quartz, and agates in an original way.

Belperron was born in Besançon, France, just at the turn of the century, and from 1923 until her death fifty years later, she designed jewelry. As a young woman, she studied drawing at the École des Beaux-Arts in Paris. Then for a decade she worked for the Parisian jewelry concern René Boivin. She left in 1933 to work with Bernard Herz, a major dealer in pearls and other stones. One of her well-known pieces for the Duchess of Windsor was a longish triangular cuff bracelet teeming with pearls.

Herz was later sent to a concentration camp (where he died in 1943). In 1945 Herz's only son, Jean, returned to France and the two joined forces as Herz-Belperron, with Jean attending to the business side and Belperron designing. They remained partners for three decades.

The Duchess of Windsor, a fan of Suzanne Belperron, 1953.
United Press Photo No. 1027168.
The Bettmann Archive

Moonstone-and-diamond bib necklace designed by Suzanne Belperron, now held in a private collection, and matching brooch, opposite.
Fred Lyon

Her designs became almost as familiar on the United States side of the Atlantic as they were abroad. Many designers seemed to want to copy her style. New York concerns tried to woo her to these shores, but she would not leave France. Among her trademarks were rock crystal carved into appealing shapes; stones set within other stones; and the clustering of gems like so many glistening sea eggs.

She often stained chalcedony (a kind of milky-colored quartz) a soft blue color, and then might combine it with sapphires to play the two tones of blue against each other, as in some well-known pieces she made for the ubiquitous Duchess of Windsor, clearly one of many enthusiasts.

The almost mischievous turn of her imagination can be seen in her famous starfish brooch, a protoplasmic creature made of clear rock crystal that holds a smaller, diamond starfish within it. For her lifetime of creativity, Belperron was awarded the medal of the Legion of Honor.

The New York jeweler E. J. Landrigan, who took over the designs of Fulco di Verdura, is now doing the same for Belperron. He has acquired 4,500 drawings from her archives and is producing the jewelry. The plan calls for the pieces to be made abroad by the French workshop Belperron herself used, Darde et Fils. The replicated designs will include most or all of the familiar materials and gestures, such as stained chalcedony and carved rock crystal. But there is one important difference: these pieces are being signed.

BOTTOM LEFT, *moonstone-and-diamond pin by Belperron.*
Fred Lyon

TOP, *blue chalcedony—and—sapphire ring designed by Belperron.*
Verdura

RIGHT, *this crystal-and-diamond starfish brooch depicts Belperron's trademark mixture of precious and semiprecious stones.*
Verdura

BLACK, STARR & FROST

*L*ike many American companies that began in the early nineteenth century, Black, Starr & Frost experienced many changes in partnership, location, and name before it became the firm we now associate with luxury jewelry. From its beginnings in New York in 1810, it sold a wide variety of merchandise—not only silverware and jewelry but also leather goods, stationery, and novelties. In 1876 the firm became known as Black, Starr & Frost, opening on Fifth Avenue, where it offered clients the latest styles in Continental jewelry. That same year the firm—along with Tiffany, Whiting, and Gorham—mounted a noteworthy display of jewels at the Centennial Exposition in Philadelphia.

In the 1920s Black, Starr & Frost, like many other luxury firms, opened branches in Palm Beach and Southampton, New York. Their repertoire included pendant-watches; "slave" link bracelets of platinum, diamonds, and emeralds; and items such as vanity cases, cigarette cases, and table clocks. In 1929 the company merged with the Gorham silver company to become Black, Starr & Frost–Gorham, Inc.

Black, Starr & Frost has provided jewels to American millionaires and English royalty, notably the Prince of Wales, as well as the Vanderbilts, Carnegies, and Guggenheims. Its jewels have also glittered on many a Hollywood actress, both on- and off-screen. Still considered an important purveyor of quality jewelry, Black, Starr & Frost maintains many locations in the United States, including Boston, Washington, D.C., Denver, and Boca Raton.

Impressive necklace consisting of thirteen graduated pear-shaped diamonds suspended from a triple row of old European-cut diamonds. Once in the estate of Flora Whitney Miller, with fitted leather box stamped "Black, Starr & Gorham." Circa 1915.
Copyright © 1987 Sotheby's, Inc.

BOIVIN

*T*he Parisian jeweler René Boivin is perhaps less widely known than some other French designers, but is held in no lesser regard by those in the know. Boivin moved into his first studio in 1890. Three years later he married Jeanne, sister of the famous couturier Paul Poiret, and together the couple built the business. Access to the wider world of the Poirets opened doors for the young company and brought in clients. The firm prospered and became one of the primary jewelers defining the styles of the 1920s.

But in the meantime, it had been struck a painful blow: René Boivin died untimely in 1917. His widow carried on the business and developed his distinctive ideas for more than forty years with the help of some estimable designers, the best known of whom was Suzanne Belperron. She established a style for the company and stayed for ten years, until 1933. The Boivins' daughter Germaine also became a designer for the firm, as did Juliette Moutard.

The Boivin firm has always been noted for its thematic emphasis on nature, featuring designs of animals such as the great cats, as well as growing things such as flowers, fruits, and vegetables. The pieces are often bejeweled on all sides and beg to be touched and turned.

Viewing some of the themes he has taken from the sea, one can see his sense of whimsy and style in such pieces as his starfish brooch made with colored cabochon stones and his lifelike shrimp wrapped around a pearl. These jewels, although rather large, sit elegantly and beautifully on a woman's shoulder or can even be admired as objects. His chameleon was truly a feat of stellar craftsmanship. Just like the real chameleon, this one was designed to change colors—perhaps to match a jacket, or simply for the sheer whimsy of it. By pushing on the creature's tongue, a swirl of rubies and emeralds twirls around its back. One can also stop in mid-color exchange and enjoy both colors at once. Boivin pieces are still known for their ingeniousness. They twirl, bend, tremble, or move to conceal or reveal precious stones—and often take up to two months to complete.

The chief designer today is goldsmith Jacques Bernard, who joined the firm of René Boivin in 1964 and by 1976 had risen to his current position as managing director. The firm is anchored by its locations in Paris but is now also at Garrard in London, where the designs are shown in a special salon.

Truly a genius, although his work is less seen than that of other designers, Boivin enjoys a special following who appreciate the beautiful, whimsical pieces created in his atelier. Commissions have been accomplished by his firm over the years for such notable clients as the Duchess of Windsor, Sacha Guitry, Cecil Beaton, Mrs. Reginald Fellowes, Tyrone Power, and Lauren Bacall.

T O P, *articulated pink tourmaline–and–diamond shrimp coiled around a baroque pearl. Brooch signed by René Boivin. (Courtesy Fred Leighton, New York)*
Andrew Edgar

B O T T O M, *sapphire-and-diamond pigeon's-wing brooch. Designed for Daisy Fellowes by René Boivin, circa 1936.*
Copyright © 1991 Sotheby's, Inc.

BOUCHERON

When presented with the words "Paris," "quality," "royalty," "history," "luxury," "innovation," and "beauty," one thinks of the house of Boucheron. Founded in 1858 by Frédéric Boucheron, the name has been synonymous with fine French jewelry ever since.

The background for Frédéric Boucheron's introduction into the world of jewelry was the Second Empire (1852–70). Empress Eugénie, wife of Napoleon III, fancied herself another Marie Antoinette and sought to bring back the motifs of the Louis XVI period. These included roses, arrows, quivers, ribbons, and garlands. Styles of the time were very extravagant, and the prevailing mode, which fashionable ladies of the time tried to emulate, was a pastiche of Greek, Roman, Etruscan, and Egyptian influences. And low necklines allowed the ostentatious display of jewelry. Many women wore what seemed their entire inventory of jewelry at one time, to trumpet their status and show up their rivals.

There is a story told of the entertainer and courtesan known as La Belle Otéro, for whom Boucheron once made a gem-studded ornament that had the effect of a bodice when worn. She was dining at Maxim's, sparkling in her multitude of jewels, when her rival Liane de Pougy walked in, simple in black velvet, followed by her maid. Surprise changed to astonishment when Liane de Pougy whipped off the girl's hat and cloak, revealing the servant decked out in all her own priceless jewels. As the triumphant Liane seated herself amid applause, Otéro stormed out, swearing violently as she passed her rival's table.

As recounted in *Boucheron* by Gilles Néret, Frédéric worked closely with the noted decorator Henri Penon to create sumptuous quarters for his shop on the Rue de Valois. His innovative design ideas extended to dramatic window displays of jewels set against swags of velvet. People flocked to gaze, and impressive clients were seen frequenting the premises. They included H.I.M. Alexandra Feodorovna, wife of Tsar Nicholas II, Grand Duchess Maria Alexandrovna, Sarah Bernhardt, H.R.H. Queen Isabella II of Spain, Count Boniface de Castellane, and the Vanderbilts, not to mention the usual assortment of peripatetic kings, dukes, and princes. Frédéric catered masterfully to their whims and caprices. He not only furnished them with personal jewels, he also often provided lavish gifts of jewels for entire wedding parties. The greater the wealth and status of the bridal pair, the greater the number of jewels given. These included necklaces, brooches, and tiaras; cuff links and tiepins.

"Braided" diamond-and-colored-stone bracelet of sapphires, rubies, emeralds, amethysts, and diamonds. By Boucheron, Paris, circa 1945.
Copyright © 1991 Sotheby's, Inc.

All the popular nineteenth-century revival styles—Japonism, chinoiserie, Egyptian, Persian—were skillfully interpreted by Frédéric. He also worked in the opulent, glittering eighteenth-century "Marie Antoinette" style, as well as the "Campana" style named for a certain Cavaliere Campana, whose collection of ancient Etruscan gold jewelry, later acquired by Napoleon III, was displayed at the Louvre in 1860. Boucheron worked in a variety of materials. Diamonds, of course—plentifully supplied from the new mines in South Africa, and set in platinum. But he also appreciated the beauty of natural materials such as ivory, wood, and rock crystal. He even used cast glass and blued steel, combined with precious stones.

Whatever technique Boucheron employed, he always exhibited a delicacy and restraint—a lightness of touch—and a penchant for the natural themes of flowers, animals, and fruit. His craftsmen were adept at all the traditional and modern jewelry techniques, but the firm is particularly known for plique-à-jour, the open-backed enameling process that creates the effect of stained glass.

Frédéric always gave his designers full credit for their contributions. He was happy to share his fame with these "co-workers," and in creating a kind of team spirit, he utilized the special talents of each. These included such names as René Lalique (before designing under his own name), Lucien Hirtz, Paul Legrand, Jules Début, and Alfred Menu.

In 1893, now at the pinnacle of his success, Boucheron moved to the Place Vendôme, where the shop stands today. Boucheron, taking over the private mansion last occupied by the beautiful Countess de Castiglione, was the first jeweler to establish itself in this area, which became the world center for *haute joaillerie*.

The house of Boucheron regularly received medals at expositions held around the world; however, like other French luxury firms, it felt challenged by the emergence of new competitors. Frédéric's son, Louis, became director when his father died in 1902 and opened branches in London and New York. He carried on the tradition of excellence and innovation, and introduced new stone-cutting methods to realize the unique visions of his designers and craftsmen, who became ever more skilled in the use of platinum. Like his father before him, Louis continued to produce jewels in the form of feathers, stars, flowers, and fauna.

At the Paris Exposition of 1925, he displayed a familial talent for showmanship with a sensational display of tiaras designed to accommodate the shorter hairstyles of the day.

By the 1920s every important jeweler was making the multiuse clip, wearable on hat, dress, or belt, and Boucheron was no exception. In fact, the item, endorsed by couturier Coco Chanel, became a Boucheron favorite. Also popular in the late 1920s and the '30s were cuff bracelets, complementing the sleeveless dresses; long earrings, which women could now show off with their short-cropped hair; and heavier, bulkier jeweled belts and bracelets.

In the late 1920s, Boucheron secured perhaps its most extraordinary commission when the Maharajah of Patiala, who had been impressed by a display of Boucheron jewels at the exposition at the Musée Galliera, asked the firm to mount six chests of his gems, whose estimated value was Fr 1.8 billion. For him, Boucheron created jewels in an Oriental Art Deco style that made the firm's fame international. It was, no doubt, the result of this coup that in 1931 caused the Shah of Iran to invite Louis to Iran to "evaluate and catalogue the magnificent treasure of ancient Persia," known variously as the Treasure of the Thousand and One Nights and the Treasures of Golconda. The horde, now well known, contained two of the largest pink diamonds in the world, a throne set with 200-carat emeralds, and a globe inlaid with 52,000 precious gems. Although Louis lived another twenty-eight years, he kept the Persian evaluation secret, despite questions from countless people. His only comment was, "Not one of these stones ever became more beautiful after it had been given a price!" The words of a true gem lover.

Fred and Gérard, Louis's sons, joined the business in 1937. Under their direction, Boucheron saw a return to the use of gold, which now was employed in many colors, such as red, pink, green, and gray. New techniques included the mounting of gems on different levels, referred to as the *chahuté* (high-kicking) style. It involved cluster setting in which stones were arranged in the shape of knots or flower pistils. The setting

Art Deco ruby, emerald, onyx, and diamond necklace by Boucheron, Paris, circa 1925. A long, articulated band designed as a blossoming rose trellis, the necklace can be divided into four sections and worn as a pair of bracelets or a choker.
Copyright © 1991 Sotheby's, Inc.

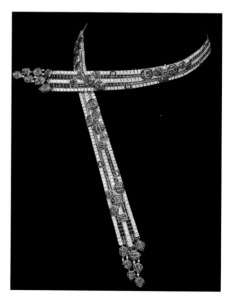

created an illusion of depth combined with delicacy, and allowed the elements in the piece to move. The "invisible setting" (see "Van Cleef & Arpels") was mastered by Boucheron but used for only about ten years, until 1946. The firm believed that the technique devalued gemstones, which had to be cut from beneath to accomplish the desired effect.

The 1950s brought ever more notable visitors to Boucheron, including Prince Philip, who commissioned a bracelet for Queen Elizabeth on the occasion of their fifth anniversary in 1952. The typically delicate design included two baguette-cut sapphire crosses, a ruby cross, rubies and diamonds studding two flowers between the interlocked initials "E" and "P," as well as Prince Philip's naval badge set with diamonds.

In 1958 the Shah of Iran asked Gérard Boucheron to carry forward his father's work of evaluating the old Persian jewels by designing a museum for the fabulous Treasure of the Thousand and One Nights. Deeply honored to be entrusted with this project, for which "unlimited funds" were provided, Gérard oversaw the construction of the entire museum, which was first built in Paris, then dismantled and shipped to Iran, where it was reassembled on the grounds of the Melli bank. The design featured a virtually fail-safe security system and dust-free cases for the jewels. Boucheron traveled to Iran with a team of jewelers to renovate the treasures to be displayed when the museum opened in 1960.

Gérard's son, Alain, became director of the firm in the 1970s, and brought with him a particular passion for rock crystal. He and his craftsmen have created both jewels and sculptural objets d'art—including clocks and figurines—that take advantage of this stone's smoky beauty. Alain has also experimented with wood and tortoiseshell combined with precious stones, demonstrating an appreciation for the intrinsic beauty of materials first expressed by his great-grandfather, Frédéric Boucheron.

Art Deco cabochon emerald–and–diamond brooch of "stylized cornucopia."
Design signed by Boucheron, London.
Christie Images

Necklace and earclip with six Colombian emeralds set in rock crystal with a gold-and-diamond mount.
Boucheron

HAUTE JOAILLERIE

The term *haute joaillerie,* literally "high jewelry," was used in the early years of this century to refer to any one of dozens of jewelers who operated elegant shops and salons on the Rue de la Paix and the Place Vendôme. Their work by definition was characterized by the inclusion of the finest-quality gemstones. (Fine jewelry distinguished primarily for its design is called *bijouterie.* The terms are often combined as *joaillerie-bijouterie* when referring to fine jewelry in the broadest sense.) In 1947 seven top French jewelers formed a trade association, La Haute Joaillerie de France, that included Boucheron, Bry, Cartier, Mauboussin, Mellerio dits Meller, Van Cleef & Arpels, and Chaumet. Over the years, and for various reasons, some firms dropped out and others were added. Today the association includes René Boivin, Gianmaria Buccellati, Mauboussin, Mellerio dits Meller, Poiray, and Van Cleef & Arpels. The name has been changed to La Joaillerie en France, indicating its openness to non-French firms.

BUCCELLATI

*T*he company Mario Buccellati established in 1919 in Milan is linked to the Italian goldsmith tradition. It trains its own artisans and has made the technique of textured engraving part of its unmistakable styling.

Textured engraving, done with a tool that dates back to the Renaissance, involves patterning surfaces with incised marks. The simplest style is called *rigato:* a straight-line pattern that is highly light-reflective. Other designs include *telato,* which has a pattern like canvas or linen; and *ornato,* which has a pattern somewhat like lace (ornate, as its Italian name suggests). The textured surfaces are then further adorned with diamonds and other gems.

As a young man, Mario Buccellati was apprenticed to the respected firm of Beltrami and Besnati. In 1919 he took over the business, giving it his own name. His customers included a number of royal houses—those of Italy, Egypt, and Spain—as well as the Vatican.

Perhaps his single best-known client was the Italian poet and military adventurer Gabriele D'Annunzio, who had hundreds of gifts made to order, much in the way that the Russian tsars used the house of Fabergé. These lavish presents included diamond bracelets, and jewelry boxes that he had inscribed with a few poetic words for a "special lady." Buccellati was then asked to fill the box with jewels.

During the 1920s Buccellati opened shops in Rome and Florence. One by one, four of his five sons joined him in the business. Gianmaria, the next to youngest, was apprenticed to his father when he was only fourteen. In the early 1950s the first shop outside of Italy was opened just off Park Avenue in New York City, followed by another in Palm Beach. Today the original salon on Milan's Via Santa Margherita is no longer in existence, but there are shops around the world bearing the Buccellati name.

Butterfly with watermelon tourmaline wings, white freshwater pearl body, and bronze freshwater pearl head. There are 38 yellow diamonds and 146 diamonds complementing this Buccellati piece. (Courtesy Gump's, San Francisco)
Fred Lyon

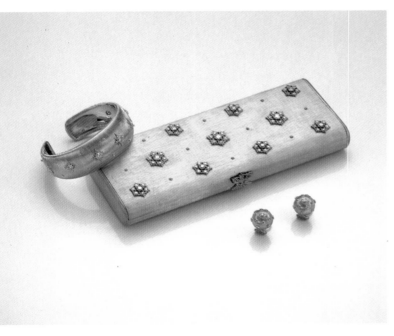

TOP LEFT, *gold-and-diamond flower pin.*
Gianmaria Buccellati

MIDDLE RIGHT, *gold bracelet with button pearls, engraved.*
Gianmaria Buccellati

BOTTOM LEFT, *bracelet, evening bag, and earrings, engraved.*
Gianmaria Buccellati

Butterfly pin in white, yellow, and pink gold, "modellato-engraved." The body is formed of two baroque pearls;
the wings carry diamonds, rubies, emeralds, and sapphires; the eyes are formed by two rubies.
Gianmaria Buccellati, 1987

Gianmaria, whose name appears on many of the shops in the international network, is also, with his son, Andrea, the company's chief designer. The Rome and Florence shops are now run by another branch of the family.

While the name Buccellati suggests gems in an elaborate surround, many know the company well for its silver ornamental objects and tableware. In New York City each aspect of the business has a separate salon: the silver shop is on Fifty-seventh Street, and the jewels on Fifth Avenue.

BVLGARI

*T*he house of Bulgari descends from an old family of Greek silversmiths, and its designs follow the tradition of Italian goldsmiths going back to ancient times. Nevertheless, Bulgari is considered one of the more modern jewelry firms, combining tradition with a contemporary style that has made its work easily identifiable.

Sotirio Bulgari, the founder of the company, was the last of nine children born into a family of artisans. He emigrated to Italy and by 1884 had married and opened a silver shop in Rome. Giorgio, one of Sotirio's sons, turned his attention to jewelry and began developing what would become the Bulgari style. Giorgio's brother Constantino, a passionate scholar and collector of antique Italian and English silver, researched and wrote an exhaustive three-volume work on the hallmarks of Italian metalsmiths.

What makes the Bulgari look so distinctive it can be spotted immediately? It is an appearance of opulent solidity, with gems set against the warm flash of yellow gold. Surfaces are compacted with precious and semiprecious stones arranged in geometric patterns that swirl or curve or meet at angles. The stones are often oval or circular, or cabochon-cut gems, and are set in bezels, the metal rings or collars that hold the stones in place instead of prongs. Strong color is another important aspect of the Bulgari style, offered in a considerable range beyond the primary trio of red for rubies, blue for sapphires, and green for emeralds. The use of gold chains and the setting of ancient coins as jewelry are other Bulgari devices that have been much copied.

Royalty and the peerage of Europe have Bulgari pieces in their collections to satisfy their personal tastes rather than their crown jewel or formal requirements. The Duchess of Windsor included Bulgari on her shopping sprees. Her famous collection of jewels auctioned in Geneva included pieces by Bulgari, as well as by Van Cleef & Arpels, Cartier, and others.

The well-traveled knew about Bulgari and had begun to regard it as one of the world's leading jewelers by the 1950s. But it was not until the 1960s that visitors to the expanded and modernized shop at No. 10 Via Condotti, along with the larger world of jewelry collectors, became increasingly impressed with the house. In the early 1970s the company made its first move outside of Italy when it opened a shop in New York City, and later, opened another. It was the third generation—Giorgio's sons Paolo and Nicola—who de-

Pink and blue sapphires and diamond bangle bracelet. (Courtesy Bulgari, New York)
Andrew Edgar

Cabochon emerald, amethyst, ruby, and diamond necklace. (Courtesy Bulgari, New York)
Andrew Edgar

cided to expand. The fourth generation, in the person of their nephew, also joined the firm. Nicola, vice president of Bulgari, directs most of the business operations in the United States.

At auction houses, the personal taste and style of the Bulgari family are reflected in sales prices, as the Bulgari signature ("BVLGARI") guarantees the excitement it was meant to inspire when it was applied to the house's creations. The combination of the antique and the new in its jewelry keeps Bulgari contemporary and influential in the world of great jewels.

And along with its jewels, Bulgari continues to deal in silver, making tea services and other articles, as well as showing silver antiques. Thus this contemporary firm keeps faith with its past.

TOP, *emerald-and-diamond necklace and earrings.*
Bulgari

BOTTOM LEFT, *central cabochon sapphire, diamond, and ruby brooch. (Courtesy Bulgari, New York)*
Andrew Edgar

BOTTOM RIGHT, *cushion-shaped sapphire, emerald, ruby, amethyst, and diamond brooch with cruciform motif. This brooch displays the wide variety of colors and stones often used in Bulgari pieces. Here, the central cushion-shaped sapphire weighs 29.26 carats.*
Copyright © 1991 Sotheby's, Inc.

CARTIER

*T*he most exquisite and collectible jewelry in the world often turns out to bear a Cartier hallmark. So it is not surprising that Cartier jewels, prized not only for distinctive designs and workmanship but also for top-quality gems, continually fetch top prices at auction. They have been favored by royalty and millionaires since the firm's founding in the mid-nineteenth century. Indeed, King Edward VII of England once remarked of the three Cartier brothers, "If they have become the jewelers of kings, it is because they are the king of jewelers."

Jeweler Louis-François Cartier, who set up shop in Paris in 1847, initially established himself with French royal patronage. By the first decade of the twentieth century Cartier had achieved a prestigious warrant to the English Court of St. James's when Edward VII commissioned the firm to design twenty-seven diadems for his 1902 coronation. By the mid-twentieth century, Cartier held thirteen certificates of royal appointment to royal houses in Europe as well as Siam. In addition, Cartier was one of an elite group of luxury jewelers whose fame had spread to the point where it was called upon to create magnificent pieces for Indian maharajahs, as well as serving patrons in the Near East and America.

Alfred Cartier, son of Louis-François, took over direction of the business in 1874 and later opened a shop on the Rue de la Paix. His sons—Louis, Jacques, and Pierre—managed the business from the turn of the century until the death of Pierre in the 1960s. Louis directed the Paris store until 1909, when it was taken over by Jacques; and Pierre ran the London and New York branches. Under the brothers' direction, the Cartier name became synonymous with luxury, chic, and status. Indeed, the brothers became part of the social lives of their clients, often socializing with nobility and the new monied class in their resorts, from St. Tropez to Kuala Lumpur. In 1908 Cartier opened a temporary branch in St. Petersburg that catered to the Romanovs.

From the late nineteenth century to World War I—the Belle Époque—Cartier was known for delicate garland-style jewels typified by elaborate bodice ornaments and by ethereal flexible diamond jewelry called *résille* (net), often rendered as ribbons, bows, and garlands. Hans Nadelhofer, in his definitive history, *Cartier: Jewelers Extraordinary,* notes that *résille* necklaces "often fitted snugly around the neck like a second skin." Some, for example the one created for Queen Alexandra, were embellished with diamond drops and bowknots. Such ornaments were designed to be worn with the creations of the couturier house of Worth, with whom the Cartiers worked closely for decades. It was Worth who had in fact encouraged Louis Cartier to participate in the 1867 Exposition Universelle, which brought the firm's magnificent jewelry international acclaim.

Like other luxury jewelers, Cartier was inspired not only by fashion but also by politics, by the arts, and by colonial expeditions that introduced to the West the art of exotic cultures. Indian turban ornaments, for

TOP, *suite of Cartier articulated tiger jewels, including a fine pair of yellow diamond–and–onyx pendant-earrings by Cartier, Paris, 1961, and a fine yellow diamond–and–onyx tiger brooch by Cartier, Paris, 1957. Formerly in the collection of the late Barbara Hutton. Copyright © 1991 Sotheby's, Inc.*

BOTTOM, *diamond choker set designed as interlocking laurel wreaths, with old European- and rose-cut diamonds. Created by Cartier, Paris, 1906. Copyright © 1991 Sotheby's, Inc.*

L E F T , *Art Deco articulated diamond-link bracelet by Cartier, circa 1925. The central pear-shaped diamond weighs 17.36 carats.*
Copyright © 1991 Sotheby's, Inc.

R I G H T , *Art Deco diamond clip by Cartier, circa 1925, set with two cushion-shaped old-mine diamonds weighing 5.64 and 5.61 carats.*
Copyright © 1991 Sotheby's, Inc.

example, inspired Cartier's famed aigrettes: diamond hair jewels that held feathers. So great was Cartier's cachet that even the turmoil of World War I had a negligible effect on its jewelry sales. "Paris, more than any other European capital," wrote Gilbert Gautier, "was living the war in a climate of elegance and frivolity." But in 1906 Cartier had designed the first wristwatch for pilots who needed a convenient method for keeping track of time while at the controls. And in 1919 Cartier designed the first thin wristwatch and named it the "Tank" as a tribute to the World War I American tank corps, which helped in the defense of France. The "Tank" was the first of Cartier's many classic designs, still sought-after to this day.

The favorable economic climate of the 1920s provided Cartier with an incentive to expand its New York quarters. In 1917 the firm effectively swapped a million-dollar Oriental pearl necklace in exchange for the Morton Plant mansion at 635 Fifth Avenue.

If, as many critics and collectors believe, Cartier became the greatest exponent of Art Deco design during this period, credit belongs largely to the brilliance of Louis Cartier's protégé, Charles Jacqueau. Jacqueau's passion for exotic motifs and colors was inspired by the dazzling costumes and stage sets of Serge Diaghilev's Ballets Russes, initially the sensational 1910 production of *Schéhérazade,* as danced by Nijinsky. This led to a highly distinctive interpretation of exotic themes—particularly chinoiserie—rendered in a brilliant new color palette. Coral, lapis, jade, onyx, and crystal were combined in remarkable designs such as the carved coral "chimera," or dragon, bangle. Popular Egyptian motifs, inspired by the opening of King Tut's tomb, were also used, including the lotus, scarab, and sphinx, and the gods Horus and Isis. The Indian influence on Cartier and other leading jewelers was tremendous as the maharajahs brought their hordes of diamonds, emeralds, and rubies to Paris and London to be reset in the modern style.

Cartier always preferred figural to geometric jewels, but mostly relegated such motifs to border designs. For the famous "tutti-frutti" jewels, for example, Cartier used emeralds, rubies, and sapphires carved as fruits,

LEFT, *crossover bracelet designed as two panthers with articulated, flexible front legs and pear-shaped emerald eyes; pavé-set with round diamonds and fancy-shaped black-onyx spots. Stamped "Cartier, Paris."*
Copyright © 1984 Sotheby's, Inc.

RIGHT, *platinum and pavé-set diamond panther with black-onyx spots and emerald eyes, boasting a flexible, articulated tail, perched on a coral branch.*
Copyright © 1984 Sotheby's, Inc.

leaves, and berries to make bracelets, clips, and stylized bowls and baskets. The effect was one of miniature opulence. By the 1930s the Cartier flower-basket brooches had become classics. They still grace the tailored lapels of Queen Elizabeth II, who owns several. Other milestones from this era include the triple-gold wedding band, *bague trois anneaux,* popularized by designer Elsie de Wolfe, and the rectangular baguette cut for gems that Pierre Cartier is credited with inventing in 1931.

The 1920s and 1930s were also the heyday of Cartier's inimitable objets d'art—boxes, cases, and frames in enamel and jewels in the Fabergé style (although it is said that the house of Fabergé borrowed ideas from Cartier on occasion). But most notably, it was the time of Cartier's magical "mystery" clocks, astonishing creations with "invisible" mechanisms often supported on the backs of mythological beasts carved from jade, agate, crystal, and coral.

In 1910 the talented Jeanne Toussaint (rumored to be Louis's lover and nicknamed by him "Panthère") joined the fabulous Cartier staff. For her, Louis Cartier created the famous Department S (for Silver), which sold original creations in enamel and silver, as well as fancy leather goods, games, and stationery. Many Cartier competitors have copied this successful marketing idea—in effect, the first boutique. Toussaint was later put in charge of the jewelry department, where she emphasized colored gems, then began designing animal-motif jewelry, although the three-dimensional panther jewels did not appear until the 1940s. These would influence generations of jewelers to come—among them David Webb, who called Toussaint "the inspiration of all of us."

A less carefree decade followed the Wall Street crash of 1929 and the ensuing Depression in America and abroad. But while sales to the middle class declined dramatically, the upper classes continued to indulge in luxury, ordering spectacular jewels from Cartier. Hollywood movies depicted an ideal lifestyle that was the goal of new money. Invariably, Cartier was the end of the rainbow.

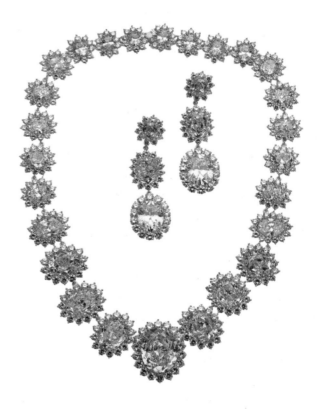

OPPOSITE, *tapered pendant-necklace of diamonds, pearls, black onyx, and opals; Cartier, circa 1915.*
Copyright © 1986 Sotheby's, Inc.

ABOVE LEFT, *18-karat gold brooch; the gold peacock sits on a cabochon sapphire with diamonds, emeralds, and sapphires.*
Cartier, New York

ABOVE RIGHT, *fancy yellow-diamond necklace, with twenty-six oval diamonds (83.75 carats) set in 18-karat gold. Shown with fancy yellow-diamond drop earrings containing six oval diamonds (26.81 carats) and 9.07 carats of white diamonds. (Courtesy Cartier, San Francisco)*
Fred Lyon

Carved emerald, sapphire, and ruby flower buds with pavé-set diamond calyxes interspersed with circular-cut diamond and cabochon
ruby, sapphire, and emerald berries. Signed by Cartier.
Christie's New York

In the 1940s Cartier's designers acknowledged fashion's "new look" and a new social informality with gold jewelry for both day and evening wear. Men's stud sets from this time approached women's jewelry in elegance. Fred Astaire ordered a set of studs and matching vest buttons made from turquoise surrounded by fine diamonds. (This set, acquired at auction, is now in a private collection.) Cartier's "transformable" pieces, which could be worn as clips, brooches, or pendants on hats, shoes, or as belt buckles, continued to enjoy great popularity.

The Duke and Duchess of Windsor made frequent trips to France, and the special pieces they ordered from Cartier set a level of style still notable some fifty years later. In 1940 the Duchess acquired the famous flamingo brooch. The Duke supplied the jewels—rubies, sapphires, emeralds, a citrine, and diamonds—by breaking up a necklace and four bracelets. In 1948, with insurance money from the Ednam Lodge theft (see "Jewel Thefts"), the Duchess purchased the first of Jeanne Toussaint's three-dimensional panther jewels, what most people think of when Cartier is mentioned. Although Barbara Hutton tried to compete with the Duchess by ordering yellow-diamond tiger jewels from Cartier (which had supplied her wedding jewels in 1933), the Duchess's panthers remained unsurpassed for sheer extravagance. At the 1987 Sotheby's Geneva sale of her jewels, Cartier bought back (for several million dollars) a panther brooch with a 116.74-carat cabochon emerald, as well as another panther, resting on a 152.35-carat cabochon sapphire. It is only fair to mention, however, that the most extensive panther parure was a gift to Princess Nina Aga Khan in 1957.

The creation and marketing of Cartier gifts—from jewelry to perfumes and pens—have been a priority since the 1940s, when the firm began selling high-fashion items worldwide. Cartier jewels were always to be found in places frequented by millionaires. When a yacht stopped at Monaco, Cartier was there to provide a diamond necklace for an evening's party; and when romances flourished in the fashionable resorts of Costa Smeralda in Sardinia, Marbella, St. Moritz, St. Tropez, Biarritz, Deauville, and Palm Beach, a Cartier diamond bracelet or ruby ring was always available to sweeten the affair. Indeed, today one can find Cartier in over five thousand outlets throughout the world, including Milan's Malpensa and Linate airports, or in the lobby of the Peninsula Hotel in Hong Kong. What is being sold in every case is an image so desirable that even Cartier has made a policy of reacquiring its own past. The Cartier Museum in Geneva now contains more than eight hundred jewels from the Paris archives, plus a collection of thirty-five thousand drawings and documents from the house of Cartier and Louis Cartier.

Today, Cartier jewelry retains an Art Deco flair that confirms the past glory of this extraordinary firm.

Cartier's Notable Acquisitions, Commissions, and Transactions

STONES

The Star of the East, a 94.80-carat drop-shaped diamond sold in 1908 to the American heiress Evalyn Walsh McLean. McLean and her husband, Beale McLean, heir to the *Washington Post* fortune, had each been given $100,000 for their honeymoon in Paris. There, the bride went shopping on the Rue de la Paix for a suitable wedding present from her father, the gold prospector Thomas F. Walsh. At Cartier she was dazzled by the fabulous diamond thought to have been owned by the Ottoman Sultan Abdülhamid II. It was mounted in a diamond necklace, suspended from a large lustrous pearl and a 34-carat hexagonal emerald. The couple succumbed to the stone's beauty, purchasing it for Fr 600,000, or $20,000. Mrs. McLean often wore the Star of the East in her hair as an aigrette and the Hope diamond (see below) around her neck.

The Hope diamond, a deep blue cushion-cut diamond of 45.52 carats acquired by Cartier in 1910 and sold to Evalyn Walsh McLean in 1912 for $154,000. Because the stone was thought to carry a legendary curse, Cartier's payment contract contained a clause that allowed her to exchange it "in case of fatality." (See "Introduction.")

Stones in the Collection of Prince Felix Youssoupov:

The Ram's Head, a 17.47-carat light rose-colored diamond purchased by Cartier in America in 1927 and sold to Mrs. Reginald Fellowes.

The Sultan of Morocco, a 35.67-carat steel-colored diamond sold in the late 1920s to Cartier in America.

The Polar Star, a cushion-cut diamond of 41.28 carats originally owned by Joseph Bonaparte, then Princess Tatiana Youssoupov. Named for the eight-point star cut on the pavilion. Sold by Cartier, Paris, in 1928 to Lydia Lady Deterding.

The Cartier, or *Taylor-Burton*, diamond, 69.42 carats, sold by Harry Winston in 1967, then at auction in 1969 to Cartier for $1,050,000 and resold to Richard Burton for $1,100,000. (See "Introduction.")

JEWELS

Sale of Prince Youssoupov's black pearls in 1924 for $400,000. This necklace, once the property of Catherine the Great, had once belonged to the Prince's mother.

The Romanov marriage crown, auctioned in 1927 by Christie's London; afterwards discovered by Pierre Cartier in a Paris antique shop. The crown was sent to Cartier in New York, where it was seen by Prince Christopher of Greece. Upon recognizing the treasure, the Prince uttered an oft-quoted melancholy reflection: "My mother had worn it and her mother before her; it had adorned all the princesses of the imperial house . . . All at once . . . the room was filled with shades of long-dead brides."

Diamond necklace and tiara, with cabochon rubies, commissioned by Prince Rainier for Grace Kelly on the occasion of their wedding.

A tiara designed for Queen Elizabeth the Queen Mother in 1953.

A double-strand pearl-and-diamond choker created in 1972 as a new setting for Elizabeth Taylor's La Peregrina, a teardrop pearl of 203.84 grains that had been owned by the Spanish royal family and the Bonapartes.

ABOVE, *Art Deco tiara/necklace mounted with nineteen fluted and engraved pear-shaped emeralds (total weight: 230.95 carats); with diamonds, pearls, and emerald beads. Once in the collection of Aga Khan III. Signed by Cartier, 1923.*
Christie Images

OPPOSITE, *Belle Époque diamond corsage ornament featuring a lily-of-the-valley motif and a central pear-shaped diamond weighing 34.08 carats. Contains a heart-shaped diamond, an oval-cut diamond weighing 23.55 carats, and circular and marquise-cut diamonds. Signed by Cartier, Paris, 1912.*
Christie Images

CHAUMET

*T*he story of Chaumet goes back more than two hundred years, to Paris in 1780. A little later in the career of the firm, it was patronized by Napoleon Bonaparte. Chaumet created the Emperor's coronation crown, now in the Louvre, as well as the diadem, now in the Vatican, that Napoleon ordered for Pope Pius VII, who officiated at the ceremony. Napoleon's wedding gift to his bride, Marie Louise, the daughter of the Austrian Emperor, Francis I, was replicated at the same time that the original was made, and a copy of the fabulous parure of rubies and diamonds was placed in the Chaumet Museum.

Chaumet, which gained its name from its director, Joseph Chaumet, in the late 1880s, served European nobles and royal courts for two centuries. Queen Victoria ordered jewelry from Chaumet through her own hand-drawn sketches, which were also put on display in the company's museum. The maharajahs of India were Chaumet customers as well.

The firm followed fashion fairly closely. Early in the twentieth century it worked in the Edwardian style, then in the 1920s produced jewels with an Oriental influence. Although associated with the old-guard French firms, Chaumet ventured into modern design and developed modified geometric forms in the 1930s and '40s. It was said of the firm that it created jewels for their beauty rather than for mere adornment. It continues to operate today from its salon on the Place Vendôme under different management.

Napoleon gave the Empress Marie Louise colored stones as well as all-white pearl and diamond jewelry. They were mounted in the grand manner Nitot made his own and which is illustrated by this replica of a ruby-and-diamond parure—crown, tiara, comb, earrings, necklace, bracelets—delivered in 1811.
Nouvelle Societé Chaumet

OPPOSITE, *diamond double-clip/brooch and bracelet by Chaumet, Paris. The clips are set with 17 round diamonds weighing approximately 27.50 carats, and 110 baguette diamonds weighing approximately 14.00 carats. The bracelet contains 34 round diamonds weighing 65.13 carats, and 78 baguette diamonds weighing approximately 14.00 carats.*
Copyright © 1989 Sotheby's, Inc.

ABOVE, *portrait of the Empress Marie Louise by Robert Lefevre, 1812 (Musée Chaumet, Paris). The empress's parure was the work of Étienne Nitot, its diamond necklace a present from Napoleon to Marie Louise to celebrate the birth of their son, the King of Rome. The necklace is now in the collection of the Smithsonian Institution, Washington, D.C.*
Nouvelle Societé Chaumet

ANGELA CUMMINGS

*M*any young designers may dream of someday becoming a leading figure at one of the major jewelry houses. But Angela Cummings scarcely had time to speculate on future triumphs. She was only twenty-three when Walter Hoving, head of Tiffany & Co., hired her virtually straight from school and made her Donald Claflin's assistant. "A genius," she says of the late designer. And then there was Jean Schlumberger, whom Cummings says she found an inspiring model. After a six-year apprenticeship, she debuted with her own collection for Tiffany in 1973.

In 1983, after sixteen years at Tiffany, she left to open her own company with her husband, Bruce Cummings, who had been an executive at Tiffany. Almost immediately they opened a boutique at Bergdorf Goodman in New York City. Boutiques subsequently opened at other stores, and are now in Japan.

Her styles range widely, from geometric patterns to the soft curves of nature. She is also known for an intricate technique called inlaying, in which flat-surfaced stones such as black jade, lapis, coral, opal, and mother of pearl are set into a gold matrix to form patterns ranging from flowered to checked. She is particularly attached to the pieces inspired by nature, and her own favorites include a "cloud" necklace, in which diamonds are dotted around overlapping circlets meant to represent clouds. She is also partial to an "acorn" necklace—originally, she saw acorns in her garden and made them into a necklace. In the finished version, some acorn cups are empty, some are full. She likes it because "it captures what I was trying to do—I made them very alive."

Necklace by Angela Cummings for Tiffany & Co. The platinum collar is pavé-set with approximately 965 diamonds (total weight: 50.00 carats) and sprinkled with blue, pink, yellow, and lotus-colored sapphires set in prongs.
Copyright © 1985 Sotheby's, Inc.

LEFT, *18-karat yellow-gold bittersweet vine. The idea for this lifelike design came from the vines that Angela found in her garden. She spray-painted the vine with gold and thought it would make a great-looking necklace.*
Angela Cummings

RIGHT, *a garden-inspired "acorn" necklace of 18-karat gold and smoky quartz. When Angela saw the acorns in her garden, she made a necklace showing some cups empty, some full. It is one of her favorite designs because "it captured what I was trying to do—I made them very alive."*
Angela Cummings

OPPOSITE, *individual links of platinum and diamonds comprise this airy "cloud" necklace—another nature theme by Cummings.*
Angela Cummings

FOUQUET

*T*he story of Maison Fouquet is that of three jewelers, father, son, and grandson, each notable in his way. From the beginning, the house developed a reputation for artistic jewelry, designing exciting pieces that attracted attention. Alphonse Fouquet, a designer, artisan, and businessman, started Maison Fouquet in 1860. His Paris atelier of about thirty workers made jewelry that was sold in other European countries and exported to as far away as South America. But he was able to exercise his artistic leanings more fully in the work he did for international expositions, where trends in European jewelry in the late nineteenth and early twentieth centuries were often developed. The company's success at the Exposition Universelle of 1878 was such that Maison Fouquet was able to move into new quarters on the Avenue de l'Opéra.

Alphonse's jewelry included revivals of Renaissance designs and themes. The pieces were made in gold with colorful enameling, and often set with small diamonds and pearls or with cameos. Sometimes the jewelry depicted striking mythological creatures or used gems to fashion naturalistic floral designs.

Alphonse handed the business over to his son, Georges, in 1895, a significant year for artistic jewels: the date is often regarded as the one in which Art Nouveau jewelry blossomed when René Lalique, the style's greatest designer, showed his dazzling work at the Salon de la Société des Artistes Français.

Acknowledging the primacy of Lalique among Art Nouveau jewelers, the decorative arts historian Charlotte Gere writes: "Georges Fouquet, however, has a good claim to second place." It is an opinion echoed by many writers on historical art jewelry.

In addition to his talent, Georges appears to have inherited his father's solid sense of trade. He walked a careful line between commerce and art, making orthodox jewelry set with precious stones that retained for him "a place in the fashionable Parisian jewelry trade," Charlotte Gere notes. But he also produced "masterly technical tours de force in the Art Nouveau style."

To produce these "tours de force," Maison Fouquet employed excellent designers and craftsmen. Georges worked for a time with the famous Czech graphic artist and designer Alphonse Mucha, and made an extraordinary serpent bracelet for the famed actress Sarah Bernhardt from a Mucha design. The Czech designer also remodeled the shop and windows when Maison Fouquet moved to a new location.

For his swirling creations of flowers, creatures of nature, and "sinuous" women, Georges worked with gold, gems, and a variety of enameling techniques. When the Art Nouveau style died an early death in the

FRED JOAILLIER

$\mathcal{B}$eginning in the 1930s, Parisians and visitors who could afford extravagant jewelry brought home pieces from Fred Joaillier. Customers over the years included Douglas Fairbanks, Mary Pickford, Marlene Dietrich, and Maurice Chevalier. Since those early days, the salon on the Rue Royale has been joined by shops in locales ranging from Monte Carlo to Beverly Hills. In 1971 the flagship shop was enlarged and the façade restored to the look it had around the turn of the century, when it was occupied by the jeweler Fouquet.

The founder of the company was Fred Samuel. His elder son, Henri, who was born in 1936—the year the shop was established—has worked in the company for many years and is now chairman. Henri's wife, Beatrice, daughter of the Baron de Beaulieu and the Comtesse de Cossette, also interests herself in the firm.

Fred Joaillier is always in search of spectacular gemstones. Among the historic stones the company acquired was the Soleil d'Or, a fancy yellow diamond of great size at 105.54 carats. Four years later, in 1981, the Samuels bought the Blue Moon, a faceted sapphire of 275 carats. Samuel *père* was also an early importer of Japanese cultured pearls. The company has a considerable collection of rosé pearls from Japan and silvered pearls from Tahiti.

OPPOSITE, *necklace with oval-shaped yellow sapphires and diamonds surrounded by round and baguette diamonds, and pendant-earrings with pear-shaped yellow sapphires surrounded by diamonds. The earrings may be attached to pendant loops on the sides of the necklace to form a "cascade" look. Signed by Fred, Paris. Copyright © 1985 Sotheby's, Inc.*

LEFT, *emerald-and-diamond necklace with a briolette-cut emerald of 136.93 carats, topped with a cushion-shaped emerald and containing 132.50 carats of pear-shaped and round diamonds. Fred Joaillier, Inc.*

GARRARD

*G*arrard, a company with a history that spans more than 250 years, holds its place in the hierarchy of the world's greatest jewelers by having been Crown Jewellers of England since 1843. Garrard has steadfastly maintained its position of prominence not only by designing and crafting crowns and royal jewels but by providing styles for the public as well.

The firm traces its history to a goldsmith named George Wickes, who set up his own business in a prosperous part of London in 1735. One of his first and most famous clients was the high-living Frederick Louis, Prince of Wales, whom his father, King George II, ultimately banished to Kew for his extravagances. Soon a jeweler and silversmith to the wealthy and noble, Wickes expanded his business. Throughout the eighteenth century the firm continued to flourish in the hands of various partners. In 1792 Robert Garrard was employed, and he was succeeded by his three sons.

In 1843 young Queen Victoria appointed Garrard Crown Jewellers. There have been only two Crown Jewellers, and the other firm no longer exists. The responsibilities that go with the appointment involve the designing, crafting, and maintenance of the official jewels and royal regalia, as well as the care of the reigning monarch's personal collection of silver and jewelry. In addition to attending to Queen Victoria's own requests, Garrard executed personal commissions for her consort, such as the series of sapphire-and-diamond brooches Prince Albert ordered for his growing family. In 1870 Garrard made a lightweight crown for the Queen; this is the one she is most often seen wearing in the paintings and statues of her later years. It was not only lighter to wear but easier to summon, as she did not have to send to the Tower of London for it.

Garrard is associated with two of the most famous diamonds in history, the Koh-i-Noor and the Cullinan (see "Introduction"), as well as jewels much in evidence in more recent days. Princess Diana's first major jewel was her wedding present from the Queen—a tiara that had belonged to Queen Mary, great-grandmother of Prince Charles. In 1914 Queen Mary, an avid collector of jewels, had Garrard make her a copy of a diadem that had belonged to her favorite aunt and confidante, the Grand Duchess Augusta of Mecklenburg-Strelitz. The tiara has nineteen tear-drop pearls of milky white dangling from a half-circle of diamond lover's knots.

As part of its caretaking responsibilities, Garrard sends a team of experts to the Tower of London for two weeks every winter. While the Tower is closed, the team cleans and repairs the royal jewelry, surrounded by armed guards. One melancholy repair was occasioned by the funeral of King George V. During the procession the Maltese cross at the top of the Imperial State Crown became ominously loosened by the vibra-

Magnificent pearl necklace—all the pearls are 15 millimeters in diameter, a size usually associated with costume jewelry.
Garrard, The Crown Jewellers

Stunning suite of sapphire-and-diamond earrings, necklace, and bracelet made in the Garrard workshop.
Garrard, The Crown Jewellers

tions of the gun carriage on which the crown rested, atop King George's coffin. The cross, containing a sapphire said to have come from the ring of Edward the Confessor, finally fell off. It was picked up by the captain of the guard and firmly repaired by Garrard.

Today Garrard continues to hold the vaunted status of Crown Jewellers, and its ledgers have been very active with entries of special regalia, tiaras, and diamonds requested by royalty. The firm crafted the engagement rings for both the Princess of Wales and the Duchess of York. When it was time for Charles and Diana to make their selection, Prince Charles summoned Garrard to Windsor Castle and the firm brought a tray of engagement rings. Diana selected her favorite, a sapphire with diamonds. The selection became a royal fiasco when the piece chosen by the couple turned out to be available to the public in the Garrard catalogue—complete with a £28,500 price tag. The episode has reportedly left Charles less attached to Garrard than his predecessors had been, and has turned him toward Asprey, Collingwood, and Kenneth Snowman at Wartski.

For his engagement ring, Prince Andrew took his brother's advice about where to shop and acquired an emerald ring from Collingwood to present to Sarah. However, Sarah politely expressed a lack of enthusiasm for emeralds; she had wanted a ruby. Andrew went to Garrard, where he sketched a ring. The result, an oval ruby surrounded by ten diamonds set in a yellow-and-white-gold band, caught Sarah's fancy indeed.

But the company is known for more than its service to royalty. Garrard likes to say that it "carries the British flag to every part of the world," flying metaphorically over trophies, coronets, and silver tableware. Among the many trophies it has made is the America's Cup, named after the *America,* the schooner that won it in 1851.

The opulent shop on Regent Street is also known for its antique silver and jewelry, clocks and watches, and amusing bibelots in precious metals. And tiaras are still obtainable. But William Summers, a director of the company who holds the actual title of Crown Jeweller, notes with regret that "tastes in tiaras are more restrained" than they once were.

Although refurbished in 1986, the shop's interior—with its deep carpeting, high ceilings, and grand staircase—retains the comfortable hauteur of Victorian times. Garrard can confidently maintain that, after some quarter of a millennium, the company has kept up its tradition of quality gems and fine craftsmanship. It has been an integral part of coronations and all the pomp, circumstance, prestige, and responsibility that go with being Crown Jewellers.

GRAFF

$\mathcal{G}$raff Diamonds Ltd. has developed a fine reputation in a very short time. After only about two decades as a jeweler, with a shop in Knightsbridge, London, Laurence Graff has become known for seeking—and often obtaining—perfect gemstones. It has been said that he is one of the most important diamond dealers in the world. It is possible that a greater number of major diamonds have passed through the hands of Laurence Graff than through those of any other living dealer.

The company's reputation for being a source of rare or unique stones has made Graff stand out in the world of extraordinary jewels. Among the notable diamonds he has obtained are the Idol's Eye (at over 70 carats it is the largest known natural blue diamond); the Windsor diamonds, two fancy yellow pear-shapes at approximately 52 and 40 carats, respectively; and the historic Porter Rhodes, which, when Graff paid almost $4 million for it in 1987, established a record at that time for the highest sum ever bid for a single stone in the United States. He also bought a famous Mogok ruby, a 15.97-carat Burmese ruby that has been called one of the world's rarest and finest gems.

Among the newly mined diamonds that he has purchased, either as polished stones or as those waiting to be cut and some day surrounded with their own intrigue and mystery, are: the Grand Coeur d'Afrique, a flawless heart-shape of 70 carats; the Empress Rose, a flawless pink pear-shape of over 72 carats; and a well-publicized 85.91-carat D-color (absolutely clear) flawless pear-shape, which was eventually set into a pendant and sold to an unnamed buyer. The diamond, for which Graff paid in excess of $9 million, is considered to be the fourth largest of its cut in the world, falling somewhat below the Cullinan III (94.5 carats), now among the private jewels of Queen Elizabeth, and almost exactly the same size as the Spoonmaker (85.8 carats), now in the Topkapi Museum in Istanbul.

Recent interest in natural color diamonds has also brought Graff into the limelight. For the company's jewelry he chooses a broad spectrum of colors, from yellow, orange, and brown through green and blue to the intense pink and red of diamonds from western Australia. The price of fancy-colored diamonds has shown a marked rise during the 1980s and early '90s. Rare diamonds and famous diamonds are in ever-increasing demand not only because of their colors and distinctive appearance but also because of their current and potential value. Their prices at auction have been setting new world records.

The Porter Rhodes diamond, shown here in mounting, is a square, emerald-cut diamond with a provenance dating back to the Kimberley Mine in 1880. It was 153.50 carats in the rough, then cut and recut to its current weight of 54.99 carats.

Copyright © 1987 Sotheby's, Inc.

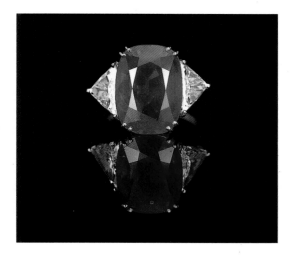

OPPOSITE, *diamond Lai Tai bangle bracelet containing just under 200 carats of diamonds arranged in a lattice motif.*
Graff, London

TOP, *a jigsaw bracelet of colored diamonds, created by Laurence Graff.*
Graff, London

BOTTOM LEFT, *koalas of pink and white diamonds, a total of 20 carats.*
Graff, London

BOTTOM RIGHT, *Mogok ruby ring. Pigeon's blood in color, this cushion-shaped 15.97-carat Burmese ruby was discovered in the Mogok Stone Tract in Upper Burma.*
Graff, London

The creations fashioned in Graff's workshop include articulated butterflies, pink-diamond panthers, and koala bears in subtle colors. But the intent in important pieces is always to have the stones hold center stage. The settings, however striking they may be, are made subsidiary to the attraction of the extraordinary gems.

Graff maintains a worldwide network of contacts to fulfill his search for perfect or unique stones. It is known that he is ready to fly anywhere to hunt down such gems.

GUCCI

*G*ucci began selling fine jewelry and art in its shops in the 1970s. Aldo Gucci reportedly expanded the concept after the new endeavor at the store in Japan succeeded; Hong Kong then followed. At Gucci's galleries in New York and Los Angeles, a "crocodile" collection of jewelry fashioned by artisans in Florence was introduced. Most of the Gucci jewelry is made in Italy. Among the company's famous clients are Imelda Marcos and the Queen of Thailand.

Necklace of eighty-three oval-shaped cabochon rubies weighing approximately 90.00 carats, embellished with florets, scallops, and ovals of 456 pavé-set round diamonds weighing approximately 10.25 carats.
Copyright © 1983 Sotheby's, Inc.

ABOVE, *multistrand Lake Biwa freshwater-pearl necklace with carved apple-green jade clasp.*
Gump's, San Francisco

OPPOSITE, *pearl necklaces with assorted clasps. (Courtesy Gump's, San Francisco)*
Lenny Li

GUMP'S

*W*hen Solomon Gump took over his brother's San Francisco frame and mirror store in 1861, it was flourishing in the wake of the gold rush. Gump added European paintings and art objects for his upwardly mobile clientele, and he prospered. In 1906, the year of the San Francisco earthquake, Solomon's son, Abraham Livingston Gump, inherited the business. And Abraham turned to another part of the world—the East. Gump's became known for its Oriental art objects, furniture, and accessories, and for its stones, jade from the Far East, and pearls from Japan and the South Seas. Gump's has become a treasure chest for shoppers visiting the West Coast and a destination for those wanting the best in imports.

Although Gump's jewelry includes settings of many kinds of gem stones, it is still the great variety of pearls—in round or odd shapes and in surprising hues—for which the store is noted, along with its jade, which may range in color from the white of ice to the black of caviar.

Some of the more glamorous and well-known people seeking these exotic Oriental stones, pearls, and jewelry have included Diamond Jim Brady, Gloria Swanson, Mary Pickford, Lillian Russell, Eleanor Roosevelt, Joan Crawford, Alfred Hitchcock, Somerset Maugham, Barbara Hutton, Judy Garland, Nancy Reagan, Gene Kelly, and members of the Vanderbilt, Mellon, and Rockefeller families.

HEMMERLE

*T*here has been a Hemmerle at the helm of this German jewelry firm since 1893, when Josef Hemmerle, a goldsmith, took over a business that had been established in the first half of the nineteenth century. The company had become famous for creating war decorations during and after the Franco-Prussian War of 1870–71. German military decorations and commemorative medals have always been extravagant, and Hemmerle's, lavishly adorned in gold and silver, were outstanding.

Josef Hemmerle's firm was also well known for gold jewelry design and for its enamel jewelry set with stones, a style that was enjoying a revival in the late nineteenth century. The company's work was widely shown at domestic and international exhibitions, and a growing reputation earned it the title of Court Jeweler *(Hoflieferant)* to the King of Bavaria.

The firm is now run by Josef's grandsons, and as has been the tradition since the first Hemmerle, its present executives are accomplished goldsmiths. Among the modern-looking designs are pairs of jewels with crossover colors. In an amusing set of lizards, the placement and graduated size of the stones are reversed on each of the pairs.

ABOVE, *"toi et moi" emerald sapphire–and–diamond lizard brooches.*
Hemmerle

OPPOSITE, *peridot-and-ruby bracelet with pink sapphire, tanzanite, and tsavorite earrings.*
Hemmerle

J A R ' S

The jeweler known as JAR's may be legendary in his own time because of the veil of remoteness that surrounds him. Or perhaps it is because of the extraordinary quality of his jewels. Although he declines ever to advertise and shrinks from publicity, his exquisite jewelry carries his name across continents.

Joel Arthur Rosenthal occupies a very small shop in an area off the Place Vendôme in Paris. His exclusive and ardent clientele bear such names as Rothschild, Getty, and Agnelli. JAR's—the only name on the shop and the signature on the pieces—was established in 1978. Rosenthal's training as a jeweler had been limited to the six months he spent with Bulgari in New York. Until he found his own path as a jeweler, he seems to have been a creative soul in search of a métier. A native New Yorker, Rosenthal studied philosophy and art history at Harvard, thought about a career as a painter, tried being a film writer, and finally moved to Paris, where he met his partner, Pierre Jeannet, in the 1960s. When they opened the obscure little place about twelve years later, it is said that the entire stock consisted of three rings.

There is an almost ethereal density about some of Rosenthal's work. It may be seen in a ground of pavé stones, as with the fabulous diamond-paved butterflies Irving Penn photographed for *Vogue;* or in micro-thin strands of metal braided into a ring. Or the quality may emerge from closely set gems of different colors that seem to flow like streamers around a bracelet. An earlier interest in working with tapestry may be reemerging in these more inspired forms.

Although it is Rosenthal's imagination that usually wins praise, the fine working of his jewelry is often singled out as well. "His work is meticulously crafted and imaginative, incorporating stones in brilliant and unexpected combinations," wrote Neil Letson in a catalogue for a Christie's sale at St. Moritz in 1991. The occasion was the fairly rare appearance of a JAR's piece at auction, a piece the catalogue listed as "an extraordinary diamond, rock crystal and yellow gold dragonfly pin."

Letson, in his brief essay, noted that "the elusive qualities that set his work apart have made his virtuoso jewels among the most evocative and desirable products of this century." And Hans Nadelhoffer, the jewelry authority, remarked in a letter on the poetic aspects of the work: "Rosenthal's designs seem to emerge from a dreamworld, and carry a secret message from an unknown land. The pieces are sublime."

TOP, *diamond, rock crystal, and yellow-gold dragonfly pin. The gold wings are of sculpted rock crystal and etched gold-leaf veins. Each wing is set with triangular table-cut diamonds weighing a total of approximately 18.00 carats. The articulated body and tail are comprised of diamond rondelles by JAR's.*
Christie Images

BOTTOM LEFT, *multicolored stone bouquet brooch set in 18-karat gold and platinum. Contains emeralds, aquamarines, green tourmaline, green garnets, yellow sapphires, amethysts, green spodumene, green beryl, peridots, and white and yellow diamonds. By JAR's. (Private collection)*
Fred Lyon

BOTTOM RIGHT, *emerald ring by JAR's. (Private collection)*
Fred Lyon

FRANCES KLEIN

*T*he Beverly Hills shop of Frances Klein Estate Jewels was started over thirty years ago. With its international clientele, it has come a long way since its beginnings in a single display case at a West Los Angeles antiques shop. Today the prices may range from $1,000 to $500,000 or more per item. But it is the variety that makes Frances Klein's antique and resale jewelry exciting.

In addition to the Cartier, Van Cleef, Tiffany, and other signed pieces one can buy at the Rodeo Drive shop, the provenance of much of the jewelry recalls the golden days of Hollywood.

Frances Klein has provided spectacular pieces for film use, such as the jewelry worth $3.5 million that Faye Dunaway wore when she played Joan Crawford on the screen. Both on- and off-screen, Joan Crawford was famous for the size and quantity of her jewels. She sometimes wore a 70-carat star sapphire ring and a 72-carat emerald-cut sapphire ring—on the same finger.

Frances Klein's collection offers this kind of nostalgia, and the glamour of such stars as Gloria Swanson, Mae West, Mary Pickford, Barbra Streisand, and Elizabeth Taylor. Many of the unusual pieces sold originally to movie stars find their way back for resale.

Fine Burmese ruby clip containing 11.50 carats of rubies and 19.70 carats of diamonds (round, baguette, and a center "kite-shape" diamond), circa 1930; Art Deco diamond necklace created by Chaumet (once owned by Rosie Dolly of the Dolly sisters), comprised of 45 carats of diamonds; Art Deco diamond, ruby, and onyx dinner ring; diamond-and-Burmese ruby earrings, circa 1915.
Frances Klein Estate Jewels

LALIQUE

*T*he leading designer of Art Nouveau jewelry was René Lalique. In France around the turn of the century, Lalique was as highly regarded as any painter or sculptor of the period. He attracted attention with the stage jewelry he designed for Sarah Bernhardt in the 1890s, then achieved great successes at exhibitions. Lalique worked for various jewelers—among them Cartier, Boucheron, Gariod, Hamelin, and Déstape—before showing under his own name. From around 1895 to 1912 he was commissioned to do work for the Armenian banker Calouste Gulbenkian. Having such a patron allowed Lalique to create his pieces without concern for sales potential. The Gulbenkian collection of some 145 pieces is now on display near Lisbon at the Pombal Palace.

Lalique broke with tradition in a number of ways, not only in using nonprecious materials such as glass, porcelain, horn, and various forms of enameling to create his jewelry, but also in utilizing the prevalent Japanese aesthetic to create a radically different look. He also portrayed the faces and sinuous figures of women—formerly the province of the fine arts—in his jewelry; used flower motifs brilliantly; and, in a fantasy elaboration of the Japanese style, fashioned unexpected creatures such as insects, birds, and bats.

Among many awards Lalique received during his life was the Legion of Honor. Although he was an outstanding jewelry designer, who designed every one of his pieces himself, he is probably more famous today for his work in glass.

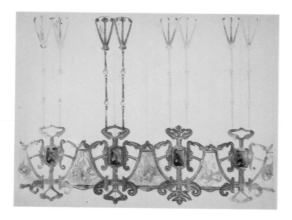

OPPOSITE, *glass, enamel, aquamarine, and diamond brooch designed as three blue chrysanthemum glass flowerheads with diamond-set stems and light-blue enamel leaves and buds. The center and tassel are mounted with oval-shaped aquamarines. Engraved "Lalique."*
Christie Images

ABOVE, *watercolor and pencil design for jewelry by René Lalique.*
Christie Images

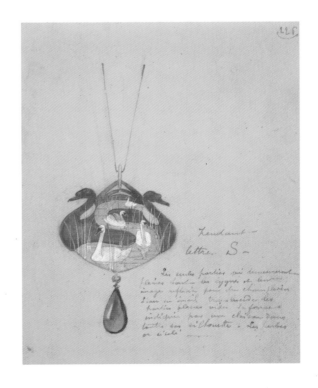

TOP, *Art Nouveau fruit-bat brooch of gray pearl, enamel, and diamonds. Unsigned, but in the Lalique style.*
Christie Images

BOTTOM LEFT, *Art Nouveau enamel-and-gold fairy brooch showing à female nymph with gold antennae and outstretched plique-à-jour enamel wings. The wings are pale green with a darker-green enamel border, embellished with opalescent green enamel drops. Signed by Lalique.*
Christie Images

BOTTOM RIGHT, *pencil and watercolor design by René Lalique—a swan pendant.*

Art Nouveau dragonfly head ornament in the Lalique style. Two entwined dragonflies in striated blue and black enamel hold a circular-cut citrine. Their engraved-horn wings are enhanced by small emeralds and trimmed to the edge with translucent enamel and rose-cut diamond sections, mounted on a horn comb. Signed and numbered by Lucian Galliard.
Christie Images

FRED LEIGHTON

*I*f it looks like it's been around forever, it probably comes from Fred Leighton." The jeweler, thus describing the style and general look of his jewelry, proudly displays the remarkable collection of temptations from around the world at his shop on Madison Avenue in New York City. His pieces are mostly estate jewelry (previously owned), with a sprinkling of some modern and some of his own designs. The latter are often his adaptations of unusual period pieces he has seen in his travels. The inventory at any moment may include "royal" pieces from almost anywhere in Europe, and range in time and style from Victorian to Art Deco to contemporary reworkings of older jewelry.

Early in its history as a jewelry shop, the firm tried marrying Mexican silver with gemstones from India, but the venture did not work out; the shop was also forced to give up its trade in fine antique American Indian jewelry because of cheap copies from abroad. Faced with some failed ideas and a dwindling stock, Fred Leighton turned toward becoming what it is today—an internationally known resale shop specializing in wonderful jewels.

The stride forward started with Victorian jewelry, which was not greatly valued at the time and could be had for relatively little. Not much more esteemed was the early modern style known as Art Deco. Except for a few wise dealers and mostly young collectors, jewelry of the period between the wars was something to be cleaned out of the bottom of jewelry cases, to be sold or even given away. So at a time when the style was easily obtained, the shop bought large collections of Art Deco; *moderne* became a type of jewelry associated with Fred Leighton. Once established in the Art Deco market, he turned to larger, more important pieces set with precious stones, and his collection became increasingly valuable.

He continues to acquire wonderful items at auction, through estate sales, and during extensive travels. Often he trades directly with old customers, repurchasing pieces they have bought from him in the past as they update and change their private collections. In his business it is possible to see the same piece being bought and sold many times over. One customer sold him a sapphire pendant that Leighton later made into a brooch. The woman who bought the brooch wore it to a large party. "That's wonderful—what a great pin!" exclaimed the original customer, who had sold it to Leighton two months earlier. "It was Mother's," was the reply.

Diamond double-dragon bracelet. (Courtesy Fred Leighton)
Andrew Edgar

ABOVE, *necklace of large Imperial jade beads. (Private collection)*
Fred Lyon

LEFT, *emerald-and-diamond butterfly. The wings en tremblant are made*
from part of a tiara once owned by the Rothschild family.
(Courtesy Fred Leighton, New York)
Andrew Edgar

OPPOSITE, *diamond-and-pearl tiara designed by Chaumet. This tiara once*
belonged to Prince Murat, one of Napoleon's generals. The large pearls, according
to Fred Leighton, "probably came from the French crown jewels."
It was redone in the early 1900s. (Courtesy Fred Leighton, New York)
Andrew Edgar

His main thrust is finding old jewelry that is beautiful (although not all his pieces are old). His clients buy for a certain look and the excellent quality, not just because the jewelry may be antique or valuable. Even in the case of great age, he insists, a piece cannot be considered dowdy. And though much of Leighton's jewelry has an opulent look, it is never gaudy. The pieces are timeless and always in good taste. An old diamond necklace, Leighton maintains, is different from a new diamond necklace in more ways than one: "One shouts; the other is quiet."

Some remarkable pieces have passed through his hands. Sometimes there is a buying coup, sometimes an oddity. He was once able to buy for a fraction of its worth one of the largest pearls from the French crown jewels because no one at the auction, he says, was aware of its provenance. He was also able to acquire the famous Fouquet serpent bracelet of Sarah Bernhardt. Another historical acquisition was a Chaumet tiara that once belonged to one of Napoleon's generals; the very large pearls on the tiara may also have come from the French crown jewels. An articulated emerald butterfly that once flew through Fred Leighton's hands was created from part of a tiara owned by a member of the Rothschild family.

During one of his trips to Europe, Fred found a remarkable yellow-diamond rose pin. Hidden in the back of the rose was a secret compartment for a perfume-soaked puff of cotton. There were channels in the back of the flower for the fragrance to waft out, thus allowing the jeweled rose to smell like a real rose. In his passion for wonderful jewelry and excellent craftsmanship, the jeweler sees himself as a perpetual "traveler"—always in search of the unusual, even the extraordinary.

Almost every piece in Fred Leighton's collection has a story or history surrounding it. A customer has merely to ask and she will be taken back in time to hear about the anecdotes and personalities behind each piece. One is drawn by the overwhelming enthusiasm Leighton has for the jewelry he sells. No wonder women flock to his shop to buy a little piece of history.

MAUBOUSSIN

*M*auboussin is counted among the great names in fine French jewelry, or *haute joaillerie*. Founded in 1827 and named for Georges Mauboussin, who became director in 1896, the firm achieved particular renown during the 1920s. At the landmark 1925 Paris Exhibition, Mauboussin's creations—displayed with those of Aucoc, Boucheron, Chaumet, Lacloche, and Van Cleef & Arpels—won the Grand Prix. Mauboussin's extraordinary pendants, in the form of stylized flower vases and fountains fashioned entirely from precious stones, were widely copied. Mauboussin used geometrically set diamonds to great effect—in bracelets, necklaces, and stylish double-clip brooches—during the 1930s.

From the 1920s through the '40s, the firm gained an international reputation through participation in many notable exhibitions. Mauboussin's distinctive jewels were seen in Rio de Janeiro, Buenos Aires, Lima, Johannesburg, Montreal, Mexico City, Athens, Brussels, and at the 1939 New York World's Fair. In addition, the firm organized three specialized Paris exhibitions—"The Emerald" (1928), "The Ruby" (1930), "The Diamond" (1931)—used as occasions to display extraordinary gems. These included a 24.30-carat emerald given by Napoleon to Empress Josephine, as well as a unique necklace of thirty-five spherical diamonds.

In the 1920s Mauboussin purchased the legendary 80-carat Nassak diamond from the Duke of Westminster, an acquisition that added to the company's prestige. Subsequently, the Maharajah of Indore and Queen Nazli of Egypt became patrons.

Mauboussin, located at 20 Place Vendôme, has branches all over the world, including Japan and Australia. Jewels are usually signed "MAUBOUSSIN" in block capital letters, although, for a brief period in the 1920s, signatures were not consistently applied.

Platinum-and-diamond necklace: 179 baguette diamonds weighing approximately 34.30 carats uphold garlands of 27 square-cut diamonds weighing approximately 35.00 carats, the collar centering 1 marquise-shaped diamond weighing approximately 2.60 carats, flanked by 2 marquise-shaped diamonds weighing approximately 2.50 carats, and completed by foliate decoration continuing toward the back and at the clasp, set with 67 marquise-shaped diamonds weighing approximately 21.60 carats.
Copyright © 1983 Sotheby's, Inc.

ABOVE, *gold, cabochon emerald, and diamond bangle bracelet, decorated with leaves, birds, and flowerheads. This bangle was presented to Paulette Goddard by her husband Charlie Chaplin after she narrowly missed the role of Scarlett O'Hara in* Gone With the Wind. *Signed Trabert & Hoeffer, Mauboussin, circa 1940.*
Copyright © 1990 Sotheby's, Inc.

OPPOSITE TOP, *plique-à-jour enamel-winged butterfly clip brooch set with diamonds, sapphires, cabochon emeralds, and cabochon ruby antennae.*
Signed by Mauboussin.
Christie Images

OPPOSITE BOTTOM, *articulated bracelet composed of step-cut, circular-cut, and baguette diamonds with fancy-shaped links at the clasp. Signed Mauboussin, Paris, circa 1935.*
Copyright © 1991 Sotheby's, Inc.

TRABERT & HOEFFER–MAUBOUSSIN

Mauboussin chose an inauspicious date, October 1, 1929, to open a branch in New York City. With the stock market crash of October 29 and the subsequent collapse of the jewelry market, the firm arranged for its inventory and name to be acquired by the well-established Trabert & Hoeffer, Inc. The new firm, Trabert & Hoeffer–Mauboussin, remained in New York, then opened branches in Los Angeles, Atlantic City, Miami, and Palm Beach. In Los Angeles, Trabert & Hoeffer–Mauboussin catered to Hollywood stars, furnishing such beauties as Paulette Goddard, Claudette Colbert, and Marlene Dietrich with dramatic Art Deco cabochon jewels for both on- and off-screen wear.

MELLERIO DITS MELLER

*T*he distinguished Parisian firm Mellerio established itself in France more than four hundred years ago. The family traces its ancestry to a Lombard family of jewelers that emigrated to France in 1515. For his service to King Louis XIII and Maria de' Medici, Jean-Marie Mellerio was rewarded with royal protection and the position of Court Jeweler and named Mellerio dits Meller (literally Mellerio alias Meller) to distinguish the family from others of the same name. The Parisian firm has been established on the Rue de la Paix since the Restoration in 1814. Although Mellerio has provided jewelry for four centuries of European royalty, the firm is best known for its nineteenth- and twentieth-century designs. These include neoclassical pieces employing Etruscan, Egyptian, and Oriental motifs, as well as the naturalistic jewels that were particularly popular in France during the 1850s. In the latter category, Mellerio created not only stylized diamond jewelry in the Garland Style but also extraordinary trompe l'oeil pieces. At the London Exhibition of 1862, Mellerio exhibited a fresh-cut spray of lilacs composed of enameled florets with diamond centers that received special commendation. The Mellerios were commissioned by Empress Eugénie and Napoleon III, along with queens of Belgium, Spain, Sweden, and England.

In each decade of the twentieth century, Mellerio responded to changing fashions with strong designs. During the 1940s and '50s, for example, the firm created stylized feather-motif brooches utilizing sheet gold and precious stones; also, a notable collection of watch bracelets. In the 1970s—the heyday of gold pendant hoop earrings—Mellerio introduced dramatic triple hoops.

Mellerio jewels are usually signed "Mellerio dits Meller." The firm is a member of La Haute Joaillerie en France and continues to be managed by the family.

This diadem was realized by Mellerio dits Meller in 1867 and bought by Queen Isabel II of Spain.
Mellerio dits Meller

MIKIMOTO

*M*ikimoto. To generations of elegant women, the name means only one thing: pearls, Japanese cultured pearls of the highest quality. The founder of the firm, Kokichi Mikimoto, is one of three pioneers credited with perfecting a culturing process that had been known in China as early as the thirteenth century. In 1893, after years of experimentation, Mikimoto found the world's first cultured pearl—a half-pearl—in one of the oysters being nurtured in his specially designed bamboo baskets in the waters of Ago Bay, Japan. He patented his method for creating the cultured half-pearl, or blister pearl; then, in 1907, with Tatsuhei Mise, he succeeded in producing a round pearl. This process, later perfected by Tokichi Nishikawa (who became Mikimoto's son-in-law), was patented around 1919. Also at this time Mikimoto began sending large quantities of round cultured pearls to London for sale at prices greatly below those of natural pearls. Through his brilliant merchandising strategies, cultured pearls quickly became a marketing phenomenon. European dealers in natural pearls balked; but in 1930 the infamous "Pearl Crash" devastated the market for natural pearls as their price was devalued 85 percent in a single day.

All at once, pearls—previously obtainable only as rare, costly, naturally occurring gems fished by divers—became widely available, a benefit to fashionable women everywhere. In the 1930s Fred Samuel of Fred Joaillier was one of the first European jewelers to build a business around cultured pearls.

Mikimoto, now a century old, maintains retail shops throughout the world. Its understated jewels—mainly necklaces of varying lengths—incorporate only the most exquisite, flawless, perfectly matched round pearls. Indeed, the company states that "only 3 out of every 100 pearls harvested will meet the Mikimoto standards." Just as the pearl industry owes much to Kokichi Mikimoto, he believed he owed much to the pearl. At age ninety-four he stated, "I owe my fine health and long life to the two pearls I have swallowed every morning of my life since I was twenty."

"Obidome" brooch of very fine cultured pearls, sapphires, emeralds, and diamonds. This design was inspired by the decorative belt adorning the front of the traditional Japanese kimono. By Mikimoto, circa 1937.

MOUSSAIEFF

*U*ncommon diamonds, especially the fancy-colored variety that occur naturally in entrancing shades of blush pink, deep jonquil-yellow, violet, cognac-brown, and more, are the rarefied stock-in-trade of Shlomo and Alisa Moussaieff. Located on London's Park Lane since 1963, the couple pursue and collect such astonishing gems—at equally astonishing prices—then combine them in truly extraordinary jewels. Only a very, very special clientele—one that has included Burton and Taylor, Stavros Niarchos, and the sisters of the late Shah of Iran—can afford, say, a necklace of multicolored heart-shaped stones that weighs in at over 72 carats; or one containing 400 carats of yellow diamonds, with a 40-carat briolette as its centerpiece. Working in the back room of his London shop, Shlomo Moussaieff—whose family have been jewelers for seven hundred years—imagines and creates such dazzling pieces with stones that cost, on average, from $70,000 to $80,000 a carat, depending upon rarity of color.

In 1987 the Moussaieffs gained wide publicity for their purchase, at Christie's New York, of a 64.83-carat diamond for $6,380,000, a record that has since been broken.

There are 400 carats of yellow diamonds, including the suspended briolette of 44 carats, in this exquisite necklace by Moussaieff.
James Wojcik

SEAMAN SCHEPPS

*T*he artful and innovative designs of Seaman Schepps, who died in 1972, hold a special place in the history of American jewelry. Schepps's signature style—chunky, clunky, fanciful, and unconventional combinations of colorful gems with natural materials and found objects—flowered in the late 1940s. His earrings of pearlized turbo shells from the Indian Ocean were perhaps Schepps's most popular design—the jewelry equivalent of the Hermès "Kelly" bag or a Chanel suit. He mounted them with gold wire and set them with cabochons of precious or semiprecious stones. All of his pieces were signed "SEAMAN SCHEPPS."

In America, Schepps counted the Roosevelts, Mellons, Du Ponts, and Rockefellers among his clients and thus was aptly dubbed "America's court jeweler." In Europe, his enthusiasts included Coco Chanel, Elsa Schiaparelli, and the Duchess of Windsor. He even had a fan in Cuba. Juana Castro saw a photograph of two Schepps bracelets in a magazine ad and fell in love with them. To make the purchase, she dispatched her two brothers, Raúl and the future leader of the revolution, Fidel, who paid with many, many traveler's checks. In the contemporary era, many renowned collectors, such as Andy Warhol and art dealer Holly Solomon, came to appreciate Schepps's colorful, sculptural work.

Schepps was born into modest circumstances on Manhattan's Lower East Side in 1881. According to family lore, he was named after a nearby Seaman's Bank for Savings. He opened his first jewelry shop in Los Angeles in 1906; moved back to New York in 1921; lost everything in the stock market crash of 1929; then reopened on Madison Avenue in 1934. Since the 1950s the firm has been located at Fifty-eighth Street and Park Avenue.

Schepps drew inspiration from several sources. During a sojourn in Paris he was impressed by the unusual work of Suzanne Belperron, who mixed colored stones and carved whole rings out of crystal or chalcedony. He was also taken with the imaginative designs of Fulco di Verdura, who was known for extravagantly decorated seashell jewels. In Hong Kong, Schepps discovered branch coral, jade, and carved chess pieces, which became part of his "Oriental" creations. He mixed precious and large semiprecious stones in unusual color combinations and is credited with reviving the topaz as a fashionable jewel.

Schepps also developed designs with his customers. They would often come to his shop with special requests and objects they wanted incorporated in a jewel. In one case, a garnet-and-opal bumblebee with

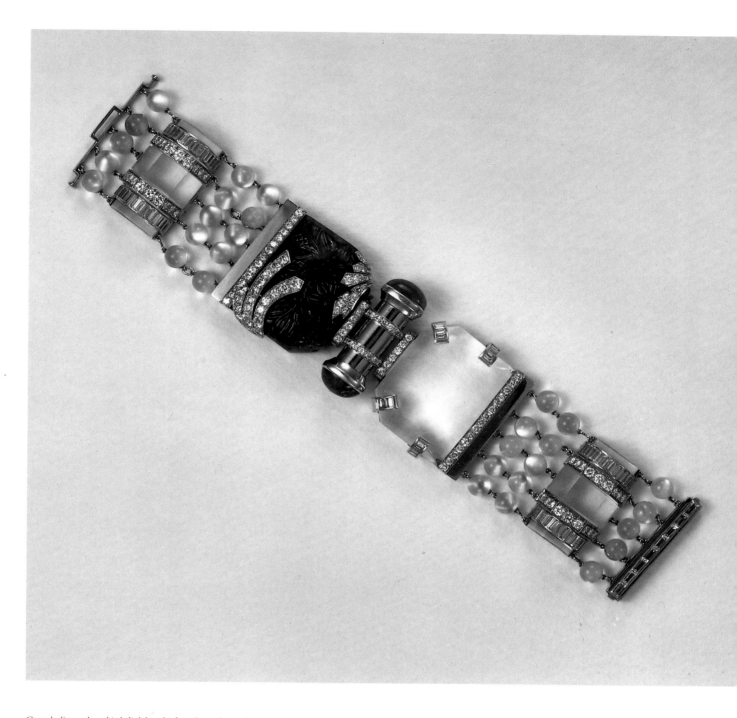

Crystal, diamond, and jade link bracelet from the Andy Warhol Collection.
Seaman Schepps

diamond wings—originally a stickpin ornament—was relocated in a brooch that featured an Oriental amber figurine of a woman, complete with gold hat and faceted ruby necklace, standing in a garden. Schepps's own amusing animal jewels—which included a mousetrap bracelet and a birdcage brooch, plus assorted frogs, deer, and horses—were eagerly sought. The Duchess of Windsor purchased a pair of Schepps's pearl chicken pins with diamond wings and heads, the design supposedly inspired by a drawing by Diane Dillon, Schepps's granddaughter.

Schepps's daughter, Patricia Schepps Vaill, who died in 1993, had directed the business since the 1960s, contributing her own designs, which she signed "PSV." In 1992 the firm began to reissue a number of original Seaman Schepps designs based on rediscovered molds and sketches.

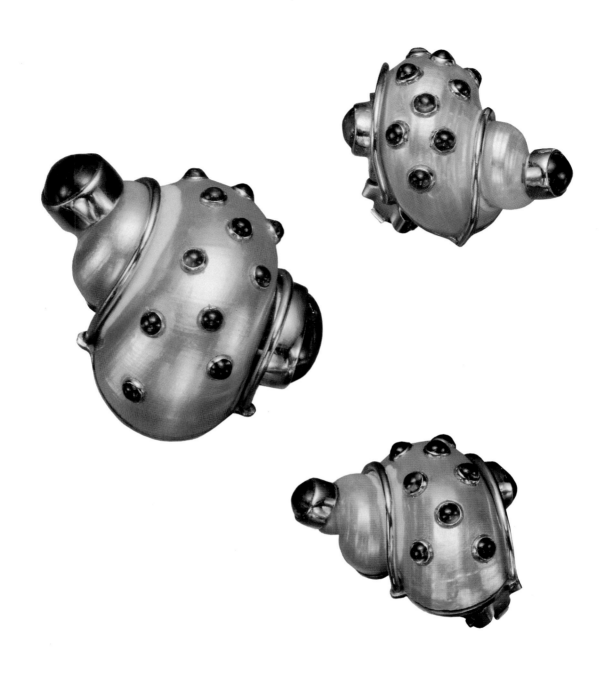

OPPOSITE, *rooster brooch of diamonds, faceted and cabochon rubies, sapphires, and emeralds.*
Seaman Schepps

ABOVE, *gold, shell, and sapphire earclips with matching brooch, signed P.S.V. of Seaman Schepps. The initials stand for*
Patricia S. Vaill, daughter of Seaman Schepps.
Copyright © 1989 Sotheby's, Inc.

SHREVE, CRUMP & LOW

*A*t the turn of the nineteenth century in France, Napoleon would soon be Emperor. His consort, Josephine, led the social whirl, and word had undoubtedly begun to filter across the Atlantic of the Parisian fondness for wearing copious jewels. In staid Boston, where memories of the Revolutionary War were beginning to fade, there was interest in attractive ornaments.

Shreve, Crump & Low had its beginning at around this time, when John McFarlane, a watchmaker from Salem, Massachusetts, who had settled in Boston, began to supply his customers with jewels. The firm prospered through a number of changes in partnership, as well as address; it hopscotched around the Washington Street area, a section inhabited by wealthy and established families. By mid-century the firm had acquired its Low (John F. Low and his descendants) and its Shreves. The first Shreve was Benjamin, son of a Salem sea captain, later followed by William, who had fought in the Civil War and was associated with the Boston Historical Society.

Customers were looking for jewels they could wear and those they could hold—scarf pins, "regard" rings, bouquet holders, jeweled fans, and opera glasses. Long strands of pearls had become fashionable, and enameled gold set with pearls was another Boston favorite.

In 1855 Charles H. Crump joined the company. His maternal ancestors had come from Newport, Rhode Island, and sailing the seas seemed to be in his blood as well. In conducting the company's business, which by now had been extended to furnishings, art objects, and tableware, Crump crossed the Atlantic a reported eighty-eight times.

Its flourishing business required Shreve, Crump & Low to move to a six-story building near Boston Common. It enlarged its offerings to include such items as special-order commemoratives and trophies, the most famous of which is the Davis Cup. But it still sold great jewelry. In 1930 Shreve, Crump & Low moved once more, this time to Back Bay, where it has remained bolstered by gilded grillwork and mahogany display cases, recognizably a Boston institution.

Diamond necklace containing 218 fancy-colored, fancy-shaped diamonds and 173 white fancy-shaped diamonds. The total weight is 128.41 carats. (Courtesy Shreve, Crump & Low, Boston)
Andrew Edgar

SHREVE & CO.

Adventurousness showed up in other members of the Shreve family. George C. Shreve, who had studied goldsmithing with Benjamin, sailed to San Francisco by way of Cape Horn. It was 1852 and he saw the possibilities of promoting gold jewelry in the wake of the gold rush. With a brother who later died, he opened a jewelry business. Shreve & Co. of San Francisco became, and continues to be, one of the finest jewelers in the city, prospering as the city grew and supplying its wealthier citizens with jewelry in European style.

STERLÉ

$\mathcal{T}$he highly original Sterlé style of the 1940s and '50s is one of fluidity, asymmetry, and fantasy. Pierre Sterlé's favorite forms—birds, flowers, leaves, and feathers—were worked both in diamonds and in colored stones; and also with a fine gold mesh of his invention called *fil d'ange* (angel wire). From 1934 to 1939, at the start of his brilliant, yet financially troubled career, the young Parisian's considerable talents were recognized and sought by the esteemed jewelers Boucheron, Chaumet, Ostertag, and Puiforcat, for whom he created and manufactured designs. By 1945 he had established a private showroom on the Avenue de l'Opéra, where he enjoyed a reputation as one of the most exclusive jewelers in Paris. In the early 1950s Sterlé created diamond jewels for the collections of the couturier Jacques Fath and won Diamonds International Awards for three consecutive years. During the 1960s he sold his jewels at Chaumet, ultimately selling his business and stock to the firm. Thereafter, Chaumet signed any of his jewels that did not bear the "Sterlé, Paris" mark. Sterlé created Oriental-style jewels for Chaumet in the 1970s. He died in 1978.

Wing-motif diamond brooch containing baguette-, pear-, and circular-cut diamonds. Designed to be worn as a pair of clips or joined to form a single elegant brooch. Signed by Sterlé, Paris.
Christie's New York

H. STERN

$\mathcal{W}$ith headquarters in Rio de Janeiro and 175 branches in a dozen countries, H. Stern is the largest producer and distributor of Brazil's famous gemstones: aquamarines, emeralds, topazes, amethysts, and tourmalines. The company also distributes Brazil's superior-quality diamonds, rubies, and sapphires, although on a smaller scale.

H. Stern is the only fully integrated jewelry concern in the world, handling everything from the mining of raw materials in the wilds of Brazil to the design, creation, and finishing of modernistic jewels for its own showrooms. In most cases, the Brazilian gems outshine their settings. Stern employs 2,200 people, of whom 600 are artisans who cut and design jewels. In addition, the firm maintains a gemological museum and the only fully equipped private gemological laboratory—for grading and evaluating stones—in South America.

Something of a Brazilian institution, H. Stern is often called upon to produce commemorative medals for the government and to represent Brazil at international competitions.

Imperial topaz of 65.5 carats with surrounding white diamonds of almost 10 carats set in black, white, and yellow gold. The topaz has a rare sherry-rose hue, making this gem a museum piece.
H. Stern Jewellers, Inc.

TIFFANY & CO.

*T*he year 1987 marked the 150th anniversary of Tiffany & Co., and in her foreword to the celebratory book *Tiffany's 150 Years*, Audrey Hepburn, star of the film *Breakfast at Tiffany's* (based on Truman Capote's short story), wrote that the store's "lustre has remained undimmed" and that "class doesn't age." Class Tiffany-style has less to do with bloodlines than with simply upholding the highest standards of design and taste. As "Holly Golightly" might have observed, those who choose and wear Tiffany jewels feel confident that they will never be criticized for lack of taste. Even in the company's recent history, it has steadfastly refused, for example, to sell diamond rings for men or—perish the thought—to make bejeweled pasties for topless waitresses, as one restaurateur requested. The store even declined to make Lucite calendar plaques for President John F. Kennedy's staff. The President insisted, had the plaques made by another company, realized his error, and returned to Tiffany to have them properly cast . . . in sterling silver.

Tiffany's colorful history—recounted in Joseph Purtell's engaging book *The Tiffany Touch*—is one of remarkable entrepreneurship. The firm began as a stationery and fancy goods store in downtown New York in 1837. Founder Charles Lewis Tiffany and his partner John B. Young quickly built up their trade from gaudy, poorly made fake jewelry to "quality" fake Parisian jewels that were an instant success. They went on to stock good gold jewelry, the grandest pieces dripping with precious stones. Jabez L. Ellis became a partner in 1841; and ten years later, Edward C. Moore, New York's leading silver manufacturer, joined the firm. Of all the partners, it was Charles Tiffany who exhibited a flair for the sensational. He not only catered to the fancies and whims of his exceptional clientele, but also occasionally dazzled them with "crazy" ideas that earned the company good publicity and revenue. In 1858, for example, he bought twenty miles of transatlantic cable and cut it into four-inch sections. He then sold the pieces as souvenirs, together with a letter of authenticity signed by the cable's inventor, Cyrus Field.

Tiffany made its first major purchase of gems in 1848 in Europe, an acquisition that included diamonds and items that may have belonged to Marie Antoinette and to Hungary's Prince Esterházy. In 1877 the world's largest and finest canary diamond, from South Africa's Kimberley mine, was purchased for $18,000. It became known as the Tiffany diamond. This stone, originally 287.42-carats, is on permanent view in the New York store and is now valued in the millions of dollars. It has been cut to 128.51 carats and 90 facets of deep fire and brilliance. At the great Paris auction of 1887 (see "Tiffany's Notable Commissions and Acquisitions," following), Tiffany purchased twenty-four items from the French crown jewels and brought

One-of-a-kind ruby-and-diamond necklace of 9 oval rubies and 159 marquise-shaped, round, and pear-shaped diamonds.
Tiffany & Co.

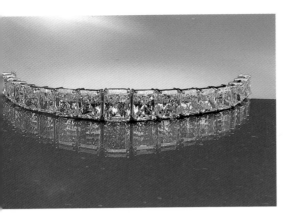

LEFT, *fancy yellow-diamond bracelet composed of seventeen fancy yellow diamonds weighing a total of 138.14 carats. (Courtesy Tiffany & Co., San Francisco)*
Fred Lyon

RIGHT, *flexible five-row diamond-collar necklace set, with 485 round diamonds weighing a total of 60.45 carats. The cultured pearl–and–diamond pendant-earrings display a positive-negative motif. The top pear- and marquise-shaped diamond clusters contain one white cultured pearl measuring approximately 13.0 millimeters and one natural black cultured pearl measuring approximately 12.8 millimeters. The suspended pear-shaped white and natural black pearls are detachable.*
Copyright © 1986 Sotheby's, Inc.

them back to New York to be sold to wealthy American women. These "souvenirs"—including a magnificent necklace of 222 large diamonds that had belonged to Empress Eugénie—were more along the lines of the Tiffany to come and earned Charles Tiffany the nickname "King of Diamonds."

Thus, Tiffany had become associated with extraordinary gems and jewels. Its fame spread through participation in expositions at home and abroad—and, not incidentally, through the invention (in 1886) of the six-pronged "Tiffany setting" for solitaire diamonds. The firm was also one of the world's foremost purveyors of Oriental (natural) pearls and, later, cultured pearls. For the 1889 Paris Exposition Universelle, Tiffany displayed an outstanding collection of native American gems and freshwater pearls that had been assembled by George Frederick Kunz, a brilliant young gemologist who had joined the firm's jewelry department ten years earlier. This "Tiffany Collection" was eventually acquired—with funding by J. P. Morgan—by New York's American Museum of Natural History. At the 1900 Paris Exposition, Tiffany displayed the magnificent iris brooch that is now in the renowned collection of Art Nouveau jewels in Baltimore's Walters Art Gallery. This realistically scaled piece is composed of 139 Montana sapphires.

Attracted not only by fabulous jewels but also by the high quality of Tiffany's other merchandise, notably silver and china, the royal, rich, and famous have flocked to the store. J. P. Morgan ordered gold and silver table services; Diamond Jim Brady was a regular, dropping in often to purchase expensive baubles for his lady friends. Lillian Russell owned a sterling silver Tiffany bicycle, one of several made by the store. Other celebrity clients included Jenny Lind, Mark Twain, General William Tecumseh Sherman, Marcel Proust,

Sarah Bernhardt, and many U.S. Presidents, among them Abraham Lincoln, who purchased a seed-pearl necklace and matching bracelets for his wife, Mary.

By the turn of the century Tiffany was flourishing, with branches in London and Paris that held royal warrants as gold- and silversmiths. In America, Louis Comfort Tiffany, the artistic son of Charles, was creating a sensation with his exotic Art Nouveau designs, most notably the sensuous iridescent glass that would become synonymous with his name. Although LCT, as he was known, never ran the firm, he was design director until his death in 1933. His jewelry, now exceedingly rare, with its combinations of glass, enameling, colored stones, and various types of metals, has been said to presage the work of Jean Schlumberger, who came to Tiffany in the 1950s.

Tiffany moved to its current headquarters, the Art Deco building at the corner of Fifth Avenue and Fifty-seventh Street in New York, in 1940; and it was there, operating at the hub of the luxury trade, that it became established as a landmark, a must-see tourist attraction, and as premier arbiter of American good taste. Tiffany was where "everyone" went, or hoped to go, to buy an engagement ring—in a Tiffany setting; or a wedding present, packaged in the irreproachable Tiffany-blue box. When Walter Hoving took over the reins as chairman of the firm in the mid-1950s, he rid the store of all designs he did not like or deem to be in the best taste; then he appointed Van Day Truex, former president of New York's Parsons School of Design, as design director. Between 1956 and 1980 Tiffany assembled a unique team of "name" designers: Jean Schlumberger, Donald Claflin, Elsa Peretti, Angela Cummings (now an independent

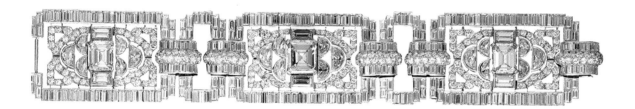

ABOVE, *Art Deco diamond bracelet. The circular-, baguette-, rectangular-, and half-moon-cut diamonds comprise the three rectangular link panels. Tiffany & Co., #11583.*
Christie's New York

LEFT, *Audrey Hepburn.*
Pictorial Press/Star File

LEFT, *seabird clip designed with 18-karat gold, platinum, pavé diamonds, blue-and-black enamel, and a ruby eye.*
Originally made in 1962 by Jean Schlumberger for Tiffany & Co.
Tiffany & Co.

TOP RIGHT, *the "Mellon Box" of peridot, turquoise, and yellow gold designed by Jean Schlumberger for Tiffany & Co. Cabochon turquoise vines adorn this compact,*
which opens to reveal a mirror and powder well. This box is number 5 in a limited edition of eleven pieces. From the estate of Ailsa Mellon Bruce.
Christie's New York

BOTTOM RIGHT, *starfish brooch with two pear-shaped emeralds nestled in pear-shaped diamond leaves, surrounded by oval-cut sapphire legs with pavé-set*
diamond tips. Signed by Schlumberger for Tiffany & Co., circa 1964. (Formerly in the estate of Mrs. William S. Paley)
Christie's New York

jeweler, discussed elsewhere in this book), and Paloma Picasso. Henry "Harry" Platt, great-great-grandson of Charles Lewis Tiffany, directed the jewelry and gem departments, where he introduced the new gemstones tanzanite and tsavorite. He also promoted the stone kunzite, which had been discovered by George Kunz. Gene Moore, creator of the famed "Tiffany windows," who was also brought into the firm at this time, was aptly dubbed "master of all he displays" by current design director John Loring.

In addition to its New York headquarters, Tiffany has added shops in domestic and international venues, including Atlanta, Beverly Hills, Boston, Chicago, Costa Mesa, Dallas, Houston, San Francisco, Washington, D.C., London, Munich, Zurich, and Hong Kong, and is represented in boutiques within other stores in Hawaii and Japan.

With its team of versatile designers and pieces from its own workshops and the growing estate department, Tiffany remains in the forefront of jewelry design, proudly carrying on the tradition of its founder, Charles Lewis Tiffany.

Tiffany's most recent designers deserve special discussion.

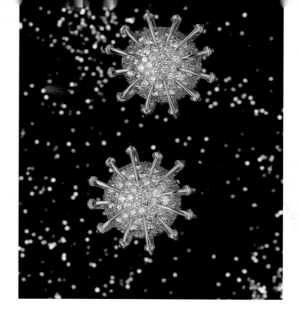

LEFT, *butterfly brooch containing 187 diamonds, 2 sapphires, and 2 emeralds, designed by Jean Schlumberger for Tiffany & Co. (Courtesy Tiffany & Co., San Francisco)*
Andrew Edgar

RIGHT, *18-karat-gold and pavé-diamond "Apollo" earrings by Jean Schlumberger for Tiffany & Co. (Courtesy Tiffany & Co., New York)*
Andrew Edgar

JEAN SCHLUMBERGER (1907–87)

One of the great geniuses of twentieth-century design, Schlumberger, together with his partner, Nicolas Bongard, joined Tiffany in 1956. The team gained recognition in the worlds of both art and fashion. The Schlumberger jewels were innovative, exotic, vibrantly colored, dramatically three-dimensional, whimsical, and marvelous. Like Louis Comfort Tiffany, Schlumberger aimed to create beauty and fantasy with a variety of materials and techniques—not merely to showcase large stones. His forms, drawn most often from nature, included elephants, camels, dolphins, bees, butterflies, parrot heads, seashells, starfish, seabirds, sea urchins, and seedpods. "I want to capture the irregularities of the universe," the artist once remarked. "I observe nature and find verve." His enchanting designs were generally rendered in enamel, gold, precious and semiprecious stones—to the delight of clients the world over. President-elect John F. Kennedy selected a Schlumberger strawberry clip in rubies and diamonds for his wife, Jacqueline, just before the inauguration. Schlumberger's whimsical diamond-studded dolphin clip was purchased by Richard Burton for Elizabeth Taylor to mark the filming of *The Night of the Iguana;* and for Joshua Logan, Schlumberger made wisteria cuff links to commemorate the Broadway opening of the director's *The Wisteria Trees*.

Although Walter Hoving called Schlumberger "the Cellini of the twentieth century," the designer saw himself as more akin to Fabergé. Indeed, his work was often similarly criticized for having mountings that cost more than the stones. Like Fabergé, he created *objets*—boxes and ornaments—with no more excuse for being than their beauty and inventiveness.

LEFT, *coral, enamel, and diamond strawberry jewelry designed by Donald Claflin for Tiffany & Co. (Bracelet courtesy Primavera Gallery, New York)*
Fred Lyon

TOP RIGHT, *diamond "leaf" brooch realistically designed by Jean Schlumberger for Tiffany & Co. The 77 natural fancy-yellow diamonds weigh approximately 3.00 carats, the 215 round diamonds approximately 6.20 carats.*
Copyright ©1987 Sotheby's, Inc.

BOTTOM RIGHT, *cultured pearl–and–diamond bangle bracelet with a flower/leaf motif, by Jean Schlumberger for Tiffany & Co.*
Christie's New York

The French-born Schlumberger began by designing costume jewelry, buttons, and baubles in Paris for Elsa Schiaparelli. Then, after a couple of stints in the army, he settled in New York, where he ran into his good friend Nicolas Bongard, ironically almost in front of Tiffany & Co. Hoving set the team up on Tiffany's mezzanine, with a private elevator. Not only did he allow them to retain control of their own designs; he made Tiffany's supply of fabulous and unusual stones available to them. Since Schlumberger's death, Tiffany has continued to produce his designs from original sketches in a workshop under the supervision of Bongard.

DONALD CLAFLIN

A principal designer of the late 1960s and early '70s, Claflin is known for charming and whimsical pieces, including the famous strawberry jewels made from coral inlaid with gold, surrounded by diamond-studded leaves. He also based jewels on characters from children's books; but he is best known for the crisscross engagement ring intended to offer an alternative to the traditional Tiffany setting. This design set a diamond at the intersection of two gold bands, thus enhancing the size and importance of the stone. The rings Claflin created to promote tanzanite, the stone Tiffany introduced to the world, were also an instant success.

ELSA PERETTI

The Italian-born Peretti joined Tiffany in 1974, coming from a career as a world-famous model and as a designer of perfume bottles and accessories for Halston. At Tiffany she caused an immediate sensation with the introduction of her "diamonds by the yard" necklace, in which anywhere from one to dozens of diamonds were "sprinkled" onto an 18-karat-gold chain. Working in silk, silver, gold, ebony, lacquer, pearls, precious and semiprecious stones, Peretti created sensual, sculptural jewels from both pop images and organic forms. The "Open Heart," the "Peretti Bean," and the "Bone" cuff bracelet have become classics. She has also created carved crystal tableware, ceramics, and leather designs for the company. Peretti is a recipient of the Coty Award.

PALOMA PICASSO

In 1980 Tiffany introduced the colorful and boldly conceived collections of Paloma Picasso—to awe, admiration, and acclaim. Working with Tiffany's remarkable assortment of enormous colored stones—tourmalines, aquamarines, rubellites, kunzite, and tanzanite—along with 18-karat gold, platinum, and diamonds, she claimed a place as one of the premier contemporary jewelry designers. Daughter of Pablo Picasso and Françoise Gilot (now Mrs. Jonas Salk), Paloma (which means "dove" in Spanish) grew

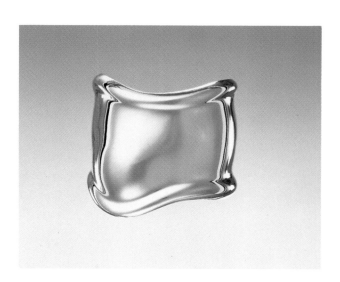

LEFT, *Elsa Peretti "Bone" cuff; conforms to the bones of the wrist. Tiffany & Co.*

TOP RIGHT, *kunzite "ribbon" ring designed by Paloma Picasso for Tiffany & Co. The kunzite weighs 52.62 carats; the accompanying 104 diamonds weigh 2.63 carats. (Courtesy Tiffany & Co., San Francisco) Fred Lyon*

BOTTOM RIGHT, *necklace designed by Paloma Picasso for Tiffany & Co., with a 118.65-carat aquamarine and 222 diamonds weighing a total of 12.80 carats. The very large central stone is typical Picasso. (Courtesy Tiffany & Co., San Francisco) Fred Lyon*

Paloma Picasso with two of her extraordinary necklaces: one an oval aquamarine with a blue zircon, the other a cushion amethyst with a pear-shaped citrine. Both necklaces feature pearls and diamond accents set in an 18-karat gold "X" setting. (Courtesy Tiffany & Co., New York)
Matthew Rolston

up drawing next to her father in his messy studio, which was often buzzing with artists and literati. After attending the University of Paris, she became a theatrical costumer and stylist. For one production she improvised a *faux* diamond necklace from rhinestone-studded Folies Bergère bikinis. When it was widely complimented, she decided on jewelry as a métier, encouraged by her friend Yves Saint Laurent. She joined Tiffany after working for the house of Zolotas in Athens.

For her tenth anniversary with Tiffany, she presented several of the typically dramatic designs that have made her famous: pear-shaped aquamarine-and-diamond "X" earrings, an aquamarine-and-citrine necklace, a hammered gold–and–emerald necklace, a pink-tourmaline ribbon ring with pavé diamonds, a tanzanite bug brooch. A petite woman with raven-black hair, white skin, and ruby lips, Picasso serves as the perfect model for her own jewelry, which John Loring has called "aggressively stylish."

Tiffany's Notable Commissions and Acquisitions

COMMISSIONS

The Belmont Cup, the most celebrated horse-racing trophy, donated in 1926 by the Belmont family to honor August Belmont, president of the Jockey Club in 1867.

The Great Seal of the United States that appears on the dollar bill; redesigned by the firm in 1885.

The Indianapolis Race Cup, first awarded in 1909.

Invitation, designed and engraved, to the Statue of Liberty Inauguration, October 28, 1886.

The Super Bowl Trophy, designed in 1966, since renamed the Vince Lombardi Trophy as a tribute to the legendary coach.

The NBA (National Basketball Association) trophy, designed in 1987.

The Johnson China, commissioned for the White House by Mrs. Lyndon Johnson. The porcelain service, designed by Van Day Truex, is decorated with ninety species of American wildflowers, reflecting the First Lady's crusade for the beautification of America.

ACQUISITIONS

Tiffany acquired twenty-four items at the Paris auction of the French crown jewels in 1887. Among the many important pieces obtained were:

The Empress Eugénie necklace of 222 large diamonds, acquired for Fr 183,000; sold to Mrs. Joseph Pulitzer.

Four Mazarin diamonds (named for Cardinal Mazarin), acquired for Fr 128,000, Fr 81,000, Fr 155,000, and Fr 71,000.

Two additional certified Mazarin diamonds from Eugénie's comb, which had been set with 208 large diamonds and constructed with shoulder-length streamers of diamonds.

VAN CLEEF & ARPELS

*S*ince 1906, when Van Cleef & Arpels opened at 22 Place Vendôme in Paris, the family-owned firm has produced truly extraordinary jewels with remarkable consistency. In every era since then, it has exhibited daring originality without sacrificing craftsmanship or elegance. Van Cleef, it is said, is never trendy but always sets the trend. The jewels of Van Cleef & Arpels rely almost exclusively upon precious stones that, in the 1940s and '50s, were combined with dramatic goldwork. Every Van Cleef & Arpels piece is made by hand and signed. Many of the firm's innovative designs have become classics.

In the 1920s Van Cleef & Arpels created magnificent lightweight, flexible bracelets, designed so that several could be worn at one time. Many of these were made entirely of diamonds; others incorporated popular Art Deco images of ancient Egypt—commemorating the opening of Tutankhamen's tomb—rendered in friezes of rubies, sapphires, and other gems. In the same era the firm devised the multipurpose clip that could be worn on hat, belt, or dress; jeweled chatelaine watches; and around 1930 the *minaudière,* an enlarged version of the *nécessaire,* or vanity box. Usually made of gold and sumptuously bejeweled, the *minaudière* functioned as an elegant day or evening purse that held cash, lipstick, powder, comb, and cigarettes. Each a unique work of art, *minaudières* were produced through the 1960s in dazzling variety. In only one instance did the firm repeat a design—for an emir who ordered thirty identical ones for each of his wives.

In the 1930s the firm's most famous innovation—the *serti invisible,* or "invisible setting"—was launched. The technique, perfected in 1935 by Alfred Van Cleef and Julien Arpels, involves the precision cutting of hundreds of color-matched gemstones that are grooved, then slid along a hidden gold "track." No metal is visible on the surface, which appears as a seamless fabric of stones. The harder gems—rubies, diamonds, and sapphires—are preferred; emeralds are rarely used because of their brittleness. In 1936 the Duchess of Windsor was one of the first women to wear an invisibly set jewel, a ruby-and-diamond holly-leaf brooch that was a Christmas gift from the Duke. She favored the firm's invisibly set flower and leaf brooches and dress clips for their look of total extravagance.

Brooch with marquise-, pear-, and circular-cut diamond spray surrounding a magnificent 65.80-carat cushion-cut sapphire of Burmese origin, signed by Van Cleef & Arpels, New York, #56852. According to Christie's provenance of the piece, there is conjecture that this stone, because of its fine color and size, may have at one time belonged to a maharajah with whom Claude Arpels exchanged currency for the gem.
Christie's New York

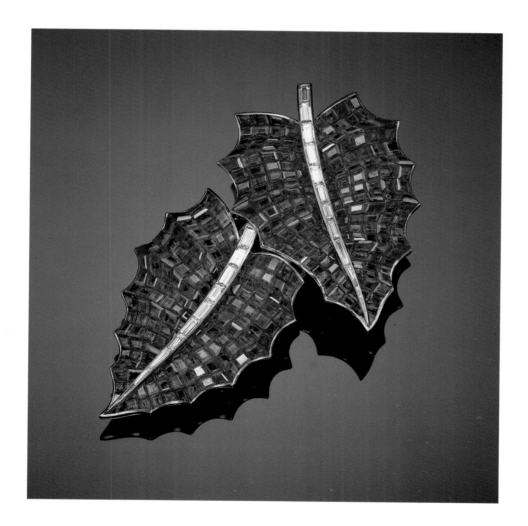

OPPOSITE TOP, *"La Parure Galliera," an invisibly set ruby–and–marquise diamond necklace with 1,444 rubies and 27 marquise diamonds.*
Van Cleef & Arpels

OPPOSITE BOTTOM, *lotus-blossom flower brooch signed and numbered by Van Cleef & Arpels. This classic VCA motif pin contains*
calibré-cut sapphires and round and baguette diamonds.
Copyright © 1989 Sotheby's, Inc.

ABOVE, *invisibly set ruby-and-diamond double-leaf brooch set. The calibré-cut rubies are accented with baguette-diamond veins.*
Copyright © 1991 Sotheby's, Inc.

OPPOSITE, *graduated row of rectangular-cut emeralds set within circular-cut diamond frames, with two half-moon-cut emeralds; joined by old European-cut and circular-cut diamond leaf motifs. Emeralds weigh a total of 60.63 carats. Signed by Van Cleef & Arpels, #NY146OSO.*
Christie's New York

ABOVE LEFT, *double-daisy brooch centered around two light yellow circular-cut diamonds weighing approximately 11.89 and 12.09 carats, complemented by baguette-cut diamond stems and a diamond leaf. Signed and numbered by Van Cleef & Arpels.*
Christie Images

ABOVE RIGHT, *Art Deco ruby, diamond, emerald, and black onyx double-rose brooch, Van Cleef & Arpels, France, circa 1925. One rose is composed of petals of buff-top calibré-cut rubies surrounding a round yellow diamond, and a second has petals of old European-cut and single-cut diamonds surrounding a round diamond. The leaves and stems are accented with calibré-cut emeralds and black onyx. The design for this brooch won a Grand Prix for VCA at the International Exhibition of Decorative Arts in Paris in 1925.*

Other prewar innovations included the *manchette,* a big, bold cuff bracelet, such as the spectacular one of sapphires and diamonds created for Marlene Dietrich. Among the firm's most stunning multipurpose jewels created at this time were the *passe-partout* floral clips of huge yellow, pink, and blue sapphires mounted in gold. They could be worn on a lapel or around the neck, attached to a gold snake chain. In 1934 the "Ludo" bracelet—named for Louis Arpels, nicknamed "Ludovic"—was introduced: a ribbonlike band of flat gold links that virtually melts around the wrist.

To the present day, the production and design of the firm's jewelry are centered in three in-house work-shops in Paris, New York, and California. Valued clients have been known to visit their jewelry in its various design stages; but more often the Arpels family has followed its glittering clientele—kings, rajahs, artists, and leaders of industry. In the 1920s they opened salons in the glamorous resorts of Deauville, Cannes, Nice, and Vichy. In the 1930s and '40s, expansion followed to New York and Europe; and today Van Cleef & Arpels is found, as well, in Hong Kong, Tokyo, Beverly Hills, Honolulu, Palm Beach, and Monte Carlo.

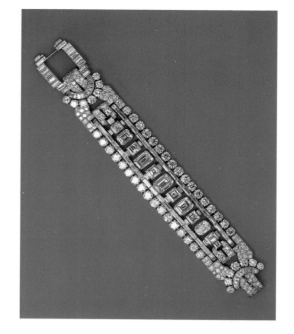

OPPOSITE, *Marlene Dietrich wearing her ruby-and-diamond bracelet, French, circa 1937. Sold at Sotheby's in New York, October 1992, for $990,000. Photograph courtesy of Sotheby's*

ABOVE LEFT, *"Spirit of Beauty" brooch. Made of diamonds and platinum, it was originally designed to commemorate VCA's fiftieth anniversary in the United States. From a design made in the 1940s called "Femme Libellule" or "Lady Dragonfly."*
Van Cleef & Arpels

ABOVE RIGHT, *flexible diamond bracelet of geometric design, signed by Van Cleef & Arpels. Contains circular-, baguette-, rectangular-, and square-cut diamonds in an openwork frame.*
Christie Images

Like other important jewelers in the 1930s, Van Cleef & Arpels experimented with combining precious and nonprecious materials to create luxurious novelty items. In one instance, a night-light of black-and-green enamel was covered with cabochon rubies and rock crystal that glowed dramatically when lit. Most unusual was a cage created for a maharajah's pet frog, Hortense—a splendiferous incarceration of agate, jade, coral, lapis lazuli, onyx, and gold.

During World War II much of the firm's inventory in France was hidden and production at the Paris store severely limited. Activity shifted to the New York store, established after Van Cleef & Arpels's participation in the 1939 World's Fair. In New York in 1945, the firm introduced the memorable ballerina clip designed in gold and precious stones by Maurice Duvallet. This lighthearted image, which became another instant classic, was most assuredly inspired by Claude Arpels, an ardent balletomane who would work with George Balanchine on the concept for his *Jewels* ballet.

After the war many of Van Cleef's earlier designs, like the "Ludo" bracelets and the flower brooches, were found to compliment the "new look" in fashion. New versions of flower-motif jewels, always a favorite in preceding eras, appeared in even greater variety, along with other naturalistic forms. It was a time of phenomenal creativity, perhaps epitomized by the "zipper" necklace of 1951. The idea for this design had been

ABOVE, *suite of peridot-and-diamond jewelry circa 1964–66, Van Cleef & Arpels. The necklace features a garland motif enhanced by oval-cut peridots and circular-cut diamonds. Shown with a pair of ear pendants and ring. From the collection of Ailsa Mellon Bruce.*
Christie's New York

OPPOSITE, *Duke and Duchess of Windsor, Venice, 1956.*
Bettmann Newsphotos

planted in 1930 by the ever-inventive Duchess of Windsor, who had requested a jeweled zipper clasp. However, the later design was an actual gold zipper, embellished with precious stones, that could be worn either unzipped as a necklace or zipped into a wide bracelet.

Van Cleef & Arpels has never released the names of its illustrious customers; but many of them advertised the fact that they wore Van Cleef jewelry. A few of the firm's most famous clients—apart from the Windsors—included Elizabeth Taylor, the Aga Khan, Gloria Swanson, Joan Fontaine, Marlene Dietrich,

Paulette Goddard, Maria Callas, Lily Pons, Princess Grace of Monaco, King Farouk, the Shah of Iran, the Prince of Nepal, the Duke of Westminster, and the Maharajah of Baroda.

Just a few of the firm's special commissions deserve mention:

1957. A parure of diamonds and pearls for the Principality of Monaco as a wedding gift from Prince Rainier to Princess Grace. A bracelet with five rows of diamonds, a gift from the Municipal Council to Princess Grace.

1965. A new crown for the Shah and Empress of Iran, using the Iranian crown jewels. Because the stones could not be removed from the Bank of Iran, Pierre Arpels had impressions made of each stone to create replicas accurate to within a hundredth of a millimeter. In Paris he used the castings to create settings that were subsequently taken back to Iran, where Arpels and a team of master craftsmen spent more than a month setting the actual stones in gold and platinum.

1967. A tiara for Barbara Hutton, with six pear-shaped diamonds, including one of 54.82 carats. Once when Pierre Arpels was visiting the heiress because she was indisposed, he was startled to find her wearing the tiara in bed.

1978. A tiara of pear-shaped, marquise, and round diamonds for Princess Grace of Monaco to wear at the wedding of her daughter, Princess Caroline.

The Princie diamond, acquired at auction in London in 1960. A magnificent pink diamond of 34.64 carats, named for the young Maharajah of Baroda, called "Princie."

The Blue Princess sapphire, acquired in Bombay. At 114 carats, it is probably the largest sapphire of its quality in the world.

The Mazarin diamond, purchased in 1964. The emerald-cut stone, 30.58 carats, showed traces of the cushion cut done in the seventeenth century by lapidaries in Paris at the request of Cardinal Mazarin. It was one of twelve "Mazarins" that the Cardinal had recut according to the methods of Louis de Berquem. (See also "Tiffany's Notable Commissions and Acquisitions.")

The Blue Heart, a blue diamond of 30.82 carats, purchased in 1953.

The Thibaw ruby, 26.13 carats, acquired in 1971.

The Walska briolette, once owned by Ganna Walska, famous diva of the 1930s. It was set in the beak of a bird fashioned from gold, diamonds, emeralds, and blue and yellow sapphires and sold in 1972 to an American industrialist.

A Hapsburg tiara, given by Napoleon to the Empress Marie Louise in 1811 on the occasion of the birth of the King of Rome. The emeralds were sold separately, and the diamond-studded mount went to Mrs. Merriweather Post, who had it set with turquoises. She donated it to the Smithsonian Institution in Washington, D.C., where it is on display.

A tiara worn by the Empress Josephine, bequeathed to her daughter Hortense, Queen of Holland, eventually sold by the Empress Eugénie in 1872. In 1989 the tiara was included in "The Age of Napoleon," an exhibition at the Metropolitan Museum of Art in New York.

A sautoir (rope necklace) and tiara, acquired from Queen Marie of Serbia, wife of Alexander I of Serbia and daughter of King Ferdinand I of Rumania. The tiara, purchased by the Queen from the Romanovs, remains in the firm's collection of historic jewelry.

OPPOSITE, *sapphire-and-diamond suite centered around a floral motif, noted as being the first important sale made by Van Cleef & Arpels. Purchased by Clare Boothe Luce in 1939, the necklace, bracelet, earclips, and brooch feature oval-cut sapphires surrounded by diamonds. The ring contains a cushion-shaped sapphire weighing 25.00 carats.*
Copyright © 1988 Sotheby's, Inc.

BELOW LEFT, *exotic bird perched on a branch with flowers of cabochon rubies, diamonds, and small cabochon emeralds. The bird has flowing feathers, a ruby collar, and a small emerald eye. Signed by Van Cleef & Arpels, New York.*
Copyright © 1989 Sotheby's, Inc.

BELOW RIGHT, *diamond, sapphire, ruby, and cultured baroque pearl sea-creature by Van Cleef & Arpels, New York. From the collection of Clare Boothe Luce.*
Copyright © 1988 Sotheby's, Inc.

VERDURA

*F*ulco di Verdura, still one of the best-kept secrets in the jewelry world, had such a loyal following that his clients might have been considered a "club." The membership included such prominent names as Marjorie Merriweather Post, Clare Boothe Luce, and Mrs. John Hay Whitney. There was also a Hollywood trade. Marlene Dietrich, Greta Garbo, and one of the Hepburns were all said to have worn his designs.

Verdura's jewelry incorporated exquisite craftsmanship with elements of surprise, humor, and whimsy. Deriving many of his themes from nature, Verdura delighted his audience and friends with an assortment of flowers, shells, and animals—often created with and around real seashells and pebbles, some of which he had actually picked up on the beach. His shell designs were copied by many contemporaries. It delighted him to obtain the shells for next to nothing and then use them as the centerpiece of a jewel-studded design, which would sell for thousands.

Verdura has been credited with inventing the rope motif in modern jewelry, reintroducing multilayered enameling on gold, and helping change the look of jewelry from the platinum that had predominated to gold. He also had a clever eye for redesigning and applying antique motifs. Among the Renaissance themes that occur in his original jewels are knotting and basket-weave patterns in metal, as well as mythological creatures—evidence of this master jeweler's rich background.

Fulco Santostefano della Cerda, Duke of Verdura, grew up in various family palazzi and villas in and around Palermo, Sicily. The design style he evolved is ducal grandeur pared down to the miniature or to fine detail, filtered through wit and a seemingly inexhaustible imagination.

In 1919 his father died; Verdura, then about twenty-one, used his ducal inheritance to live well in Paris, Venice, and Cannes for seven fat years. Legend has it that the enormous and lavish fancy dress ball he gave at the old palazzo cost him the last of his patrimony. In 1926 he left for Paris to seek a career that would utilize his artistic flair.

He became a textile designer for Coco Chanel; after six months' exposure to his impressive talent, she made him head of her jewelry department. He designed for her a pair of black-and-white enamel bracelets set with jeweled Maltese crosses; the couturier made them famous by wearing them constantly.

Unusual multicolor leaf brooch combining sapphires, zircons, alousites, and tourmaline.
Verdura

LEFT TOP, *citrine, emerald, and diamond pineapple pin. (Courtesy Verdura)*
Andrew Edgar

LEFT BOTTOM, *multistrand peridot-bead necklace with diamond tassel clasp.*
James Wojcik

RIGHT, *pearl-and-diamond mouse pin. (Courtesy Verdura)*
Andrew Edgar

In 1934 Verdura traveled to the United States in search of fame and fortune, and added another circle of the rich and famous to his loyal band of friends. Elsa Maxwell once put him on a list of the top dozen people to form the perfect dinner party because of his charm, wit, and erudition. Verdura worked as chief designer for Paul Flato in both New York and Los Angeles until 1939. He then started his own business in New York—in a suite once occupied by Cartier—with the moral and financial support of his good friends Cole and Linda Porter, whom he had met in Venice in the 1920s and with whom he maintained a close friendship over the years.

In addition to his innovations in jewelry, Verdura made a contribution to the fashion industry with his collection of hat clips, which were highly versatile.

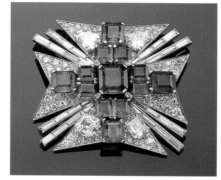

LEFT, *cabochon amethyst, diamond, and yellow-gold heart brooch by Verdura.*
Christie's New York

RIGHT, *emerald-and-diamond Maltese-cross brooch, circa 1945. Cross motif formed of emerald-cut emeralds and diamonds; further decorated with pavé-set round and baguette diamonds, mounted in platinum by Verdura.*
Copyright © 1988 Sotheby's, Inc.

Verdura designed his jewelry the same way he conducted himself in the social arena—with wit and impeccable style. Neil Letson, the jewelry writer and historian, wrote about a now-famous anecdote concerning Verdura and the Duchess of Windsor, recounting that she "once took a topaz rose in delicately shaded pink and green stones from his shop and wore it (without having paid for it), telling her friends that it was her own design. Later she returned it to Fulco and asked to exchange it for a topaz thistle—one of her husband's emblems. 'I am so sorry,' he told the Duchess, 'I'd love to but, alas, I can't. Everything here is designed by me, and I understand that this rose is your design.' "

In the early 1970s Verdura sold his business to an associate and retired to London, where he painted tiny miniatures, saw friends, and wrote a memoir of his childhood. He died in 1978. Today E. J. Landrigan is the owner and producer of Verdura's designs, and says he delights in the multitude of finely detailed gouache jewelry sketches he now controls. He often seeks out Verdura pieces at auctions (signed "Verdura" in small block letters) and from old-time Verdura customers. He tries to conduct the business in the same gentlemanly fashion as its founder did.

OPPOSITE, *multistrand necklace of iolite beads and green tourmaline, with a sapphire pendant.*
Verdura

ABOVE, *flower brooch centered around two heart-shaped pink topazes weighing approximately 20.00 carats,*
decorated with a spray of diamond flowers, a butterfly, and a bee. By Verdura.
Copyright © 1983 Sotheby's, Inc.

ABOVE, *emerald-and-sapphire paisley earrings/brooches with detachable drops, containing 35.24 carats of sapphires and 23.72 carats of emeralds.*
(Private collection, Switzerland)
Christopher Walling/New York

OPPOSITE, *trademark "X" pearl–and–pavé diamond bracelet with cabochon rubies. (Private collection, Hawaii)*
Christopher Walling/New York

CHRISTOPHER WALLING

$\mathscr{R}$omancing the pearl is what New York jeweler Christopher Walling does best. Walling calls the pearl "the only gem that seems alive, a chameleon whose soft glow interacts with and highlights the best features of its wearer and other gems." Since 1980 his trademark design has been the pearl "kiss," which is an X-shaped cultured baroque pearl that he treats in many splendored ways: set in high gold bezels, or collars; paired with large colored stones; trellised with exquisite strands of pavé emeralds.

When Walling first espoused the pearl, he used lustrous freshwater specimens from Japan's Lake Biwa. But as pollution adversely affected the quality and availability of this source, he turned to large South Seas saltwater pearls from Tahiti and Australia. This locale yields both the shimmering white and the iridescent black pearls that Walling also uses to great effect.

In the late 1980s the scarcity of high-quality pearls led Walling to focus increasingly on diamonds and colored stones and to explore new forms. The famous "X" jewel became available in pavé diamonds; and a collection utilizing pink diamonds from Australia's Argyle mines yielded naturalistic floral jewels.

In the 1990s Walling introduced double paisley earrings made entirely of emeralds and sapphires that, in both form and color, are his tribute to India's famed blue-green esthetic. Such purity of solid color first impressed European jewelers around 1900, when the maharajahs brought the contents of their jewel chests to Paris and London for resetting.

Attracted both to archaeology and jewelry design since childhood, Walling cites many historical influences on his work, from Elizabethan and Renaissance baroque-pearl jewels to eighteenth-century *objets de vertu* in Dresden's famed Green Vaults. He also cites Suzanne Belperron, whom he considers his mentor and whom he calls "the best designer of the twentieth century." (See "Belperron.")

Walling, a new force in pearl design and in the jewelry world, signs his work "C. WALLING."

DAVID WEBB

*J*ust as Harry Winston means spectacular diamonds, and Van Cleef & Arpels is famed for invisibly set gemstones, David Webb's name became, in postwar America, synonymous with bold, colorful "daytime jewelry." Catering to fashionable women who sought designs that could be worn at any time, Webb worked with large cabochon stones, carved crystal, enameling, and animal forms to create a signature style. Born in North Carolina in 1925, Webb established his firm in New York City in 1948 with partner Nina Silberstein. At Webb's death in 1975, Silberstein became president of the firm and chief designer.

Webb's famous line of animal jewelry was dubbed the "enamel jungle" by *Vogue* magazine in the 1960s. Citing as inspiration both the eighteenth-century enameled jewelry of eastern India and the animal jewels of Cartier's Jeanne Toussaint, Webb sculpted his menagerie in 18-karat gold. Enamel-and-jewel combinations sometimes copied realistic colors (panda bracelets of black enamel and mother of pearl, for example, that Webb created after studying pandas at the zoo; or green frogs with ruby eyes; or black-and-yellow-striped tigers with emerald eyes). But Webb designs also were often fantastical, like a dolphin carved from azurmalachite with a mouth full of pavé diamonds. Such creatures appealed not only to Webb's clients (the Duchess of Windsor received a frog bracelet from the Duke in 1964) but also to other jewelers, some of whom have shamelessly copied the style.

Like Seaman Schepps, Fulco di Verdura, and Darde et Fils of Paris, David Webb also made jewels from seashells decorated with gemstones. The Duchess of Windsor owned Webb earclips made from striped snail shells set in gold and mounted with coral and turquoise.

Webb's more conventional cluster jewels reveal an Art Deco influence in their pairing of rock crystal and coral with diamonds and other precious gems; but boldly scaled 18-karat-gold settings are a clue to postwar modern taste.

Several American Presidents have commissioned David Webb to create state gifts. Perhaps the most extravagant was a 14-karat-gold model of the White House that Richard Nixon gave to Eisaku Sato, Japan's Prime Minister. John F. Kennedy also gave gifts by Webb, but he asked for objects made from native American materials, Arizona azurite or Arkansas citrine, for example.

Torsade necklace of gray and pinkish-gray freshwater pearls by David Webb, with a butterfly clasp decorated with diamonds, emeralds, sapphires, and rubies, and a detachable pear-shaped ruby drop. The butterfly can be detached from the necklace to be worn as a brooch. Once in the collection of Françoise and Oscar de la Renta. Copyright © 1985 Sotheby's, Inc.

LEFT, *frog bangle bracelet of green enamel, rubies, and diamonds by David Webb.*
Copyright © 1991 Sotheby's, Inc.

RIGHT TOP, *diamond pin. One of Webb's elegant clients took her Bulgari diamond ring, pin, and bracelet to David Webb and asked him to "create the most beautiful sunburst" for her. The resulting pin was worn by the lady for the first time at the Truman Capote black-and-white ball. (Private collection)*
Fred Lyon

RIGHT BOTTOM, *cabochon emerald–and–diamond ring by David Webb. (Private collection)*
Fred Lyon

OPPOSITE, *platinum-and-diamond pendant-necklace by David Webb.*
Copyright © 1983 Sotheby's, Inc.

Nina Silberstein, in carrying on the tradition, continues to work with colored stones that epitomize the Webb style. And she continues to supply Webb's own carnival of animal jewels to an appreciative, if sometimes eccentric, clientele. A prime example was several years ago, when David Webb was alive and a famous singer-actress-director was considering purchase of a bracelet. While she and Webb were discussing the piece, she gave it to her dog to play with. Webb calmly told her that the item was "still ours" until it was paid for. So she wrote a check and left with the dog still holding the bracelet in its mouth. "I guess," mused Silberstein, "when you are known for animal jewels, some people take it to mean just that."

HARRY WINSTON

*H*arry Winston devoted most of his long life to the world of gems, especially diamonds. He was working in the jewelry business by the time he was fifteen. A few years later, with $2,000 he had saved, he opened his own diamond company, acting as broker, importer, and jeweler.

Before he had reached thirty, he was dealing in estate jewelry collections worth millions—having understood that these old-fashioned jewels in their archaic settings were an underpriced source of wonderful stones. He removed gems, recut them and reset them in ways that gave them a modern look.

He said once, "My father was always afraid that jewels would some day possess me. Sometimes I think he was right." One wonders what the elder Winston, a modest retail jeweler, would have thought of the son who came to be called the "King of Diamonds"—the second king, since it was also an appellation given in the nineteenth century to Charles Lewis Tiffany.

Winston was so thoroughly associated with great diamonds that even Marilyn Monroe invoked his name in the film *Gentlemen Prefer Blondes:* "Talk to me, Harry Winston, tell me all about it," she cooed in her song about diamonds being a girl's best friend. Serious jewelry collectors have looked to the house of Harry Winston for their best diamonds since the company was established at a fashionable address on Fifth Avenue in 1932. Winston, who was born toward the end of the nineteenth century, was also one of the first American jewelers in Europe. Over the years Harry Winston acquired magnificent and storied stones. He held more than 60 of the world's 303 major diamonds, probably more than any other individual, government, or royal house. Although known primarily for his diamonds, he also held some of the world's finest rubies, emeralds, sapphires, and pearls. From the start, Winston's reputation was built on high-quality stones worked with impeccable craftsmanship.

His design style emphasized the sheer beauty of the stones. He cut for brilliancy and placed the jewels in light settings, often displaying gems in opulent clusters. His innovative three-dimensional arrangement of precious stones focused attention on the jewels rather than on the metal. It was an approach to jewelry design that became distinctively his. Winston tried to be discreet about his exclusive clientele, but his brilliant and unique gems often gave him away when the owners wore them. Winston's creations adorned Broadway and Hollywood's brightest stars, and society and royal families as well.

Diamond necklace. All stones are D-color and internally flawless, with a total weight of 199 carats. By Harry Winston.
Harry Winston, Inc.

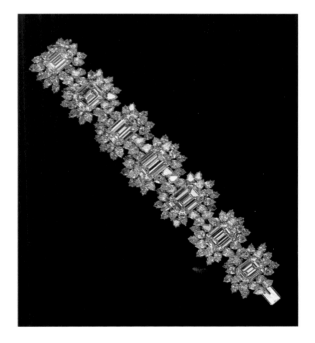

OPPOSITE, *looping brooch of baguette-cut diamond scrolls and sprays suspending a very light blue pear-shaped diamond weighing approximately 10.15 carats and two near colorless pear-shaped diamonds. Formerly in the collection of Elizabeth Parke Firestone. Signed by Harry Winston.*
Christie's New York

ABOVE LEFT TOP, *emerald and diamond earclips. The two perfectly matched pear-shaped Colombian emeralds (total carat weight: 45.67) exhibit the finest size and color that Colombia has to offer. The emeralds are decorated on top and surrounded by pear- and marquise-shaped diamonds. The detachable pendants are by Harry Winston.*
Copyright © 1987 Sotheby's, Inc.

ABOVE RIGHT TOP, *Marisa Berenson in a photograph taken for the National Geographic Society special entitled "Splendid Stones." (Courtesy National Geographic Society)*
Berry Berenson

ABOVE RIGHT BOTTOM, *bracelet composed of seven rectangular-cut diamonds (carat weights: 9.09, 13.44, 12.86, 18.18, 13.58, 15.94, and 9.11) surrounded by floral clusters of pear-shaped diamonds.*
Christie Images

LEFT, *ring with a 29.63-carat emerald-cut emerald and baguette side diamonds set in platinum. Signed by Harry Winston.*
Copyright © 1988 Sotheby's, Inc.

RIGHT, *ring with a cushion-shaped 43.22 carat sapphire of Burmese origin flanked by baguette-cut diamonds. By Harry Winston.*
Christie Images

OPPOSITE, *diamond-chandelier pendant-earclips, Harry Winston, 1961. Elongated pear-shaped diamonds weigh 15.90 and 15.50 carats, complemented by pear, marquise, and round diamonds weighing approximately 48.75 carats. Large pear-shaped diamonds are detachable. From the estate of the late Mrs. Harry Winston.*
Copyright © 1992 Sotheby's, Inc.

In addition to an instinctive eye for great stones (it is said that as a young man he bought a genuine emerald in a junk shop for a quarter), he knew how to acquire. One of his major sources was De Beers Consolidated Mines Ltd. In 1974 Winston bought $24.5 million in rough diamonds, which at that point was the largest single sale ever transacted. When Winston asked for "a little something to sweeten the deal," Harry Oppenheimer, head of De Beers, pulled a 181-carat rough gem out of his pocket and rolled it toward Winston. It was named the Deal Sweetener.

Harry Winston also knew how to sell. A generally good judge of people, he knew how to handle his clients, from famous ones to young potential buyers. He knew when to allow a client to keep a piece of jewelry overnight, and how to romance the lover of stones. In 1948 he wrote to the Duchess of Windsor (not surprisingly, a major customer), saying that he was sending along two canary-diamond clips. The stones weighed a hefty 92.92 carats and "are priceless!" he told her, adding that "never before in my experience have I seen a pair of pear-shaped canary diamonds so wonderfully matched . . . It is due only to existing conditions in the world today that we were able to purchase diamonds such as these from old estates of royalty. In fact, they are so magnificent," he wrote, "that were it not you I am offering them to—I should keep them here as showpieces."

She replied four days later: "I can't think of anything I would rather have than these two diamonds. I have worn them twice and they have caused a sensation . . . I would of course have to have two medium-size yellow diamond earrings . . . If you have anything that might do would you send them down as I have nothing suitable."

Winston, who died in 1978, prided himself both on his understanding of people and on his knowledge of stones.

The company is rare among high-fashion jewelers in that it maintains high-level wholesale and manufacturing operations in addition to its retail salons. The cutting of rough diamonds, and the polishing, designing, and creation of jewels, are all done in Winston's New York building on Fifth Avenue, currently inhabited by the company's third generation of jewelers. The company has handled some of the world's largest and best-known diamonds, including the legendary Hope (see "Introduction").

Harry Winston's biographer, Laurence S. Krashes, wrote: "No king, nawab, or emperor ever possessed more diamond treasure in his life." Talking about the diamond business, Harry Winston himself once said: "It's a Cinderella world. It has everything—people, drama, romance, precious stones, speculation, excitement. What more could you want?"

Some of Harry Winston's Notable Acquisitions

DIAMONDS

The Jonker was the seventh-largest rough diamond ever found. The unusually clear, pure stone was unearthed near Pretoria, South Africa, on the farm of Jacobus Jonker. When Harry Winston bought it in London in 1935, a debate ensued as to how to get the 726-carat stone safely back to the United States. Winston finally sent it by ordinary registered mail for 64 cents postage.

The huge gem, the first major stone to be cleft in this country, was cut into twelve stones. The largest one, named the Jonker, was cut again two years later, ending up as an oblong emerald-cut with a weight of 125.35 carats. Winston was so fond of the stone, which he displayed at charity exhibitions, that he held on to it for sixteen years, finally selling it in 1951 to King Farouk of Egypt.

The Lal Qila was named after a great imperial palace-fort built by the Mogul ruler Shah Jahan, who also built the Taj Mahal. Winston bought the 70-carat deep green diamond from an Indian dealer and lent it, on memorandum, to that avid collector of jewels, King Farouk. But when the King was overthrown in 1952, the stone—unpaid for—disappeared from public view and has not been sighted since.

The Mabel Boll, a 46.57-carat emerald-cut diamond, got its name from a beautiful Broadway performer of the 1920s who earned her sobriquet of "Queen of Diamonds" by frequently wearing all her jewels in public, often almost half a million dollars' worth on one hand alone. The Boll diamond was one of many gifts of jewelry to Mabel from one of her many husbands, a Colombian coffee tycoon.

The Martian Pink was appreciably smaller than other major stones in the Winston inventory, but it was notable for the intensity of its color. When the United States launched a satellite on a mission to photograph Mars in 1976, Harry Winston had the 12-carat pink gem on hand; it was named for the red planet.

The Star of Independence was cut by Harry Winston in 1976 from a 204-carat rough diamond to a 75.52-carat pear-shape. As it was the year of the American bicentennial celebration, Ronald Winston, Harry's son and later head of the company, gave it a commemorative name; a few weeks later it brought a price of more than $4 million. Ronald is the third generation of Winstons in the jewelry business.

The Star of Sierra Leone was discovered in 1972; the 969-carat rough stone was one of the largest diamonds ever found. Winston bought it and had it cut into eleven stones, the biggest of which was a 143.20-carat emerald-cut. But the beautiful gem was flawed. He ordered it recut, and gained six gems—the largest of which was a perfect pear-shape of 54 carats—that were arranged in a brooch like the petals of a flower. The remaining gem was a flawless, clear-color emerald-cut of 35.52 carats, subsequently known as the Star of Sierra Leone No. 2.

The President Vargas in its rough state was six-tenths of a carat larger than the Jonker. Found in Brazil in 1938, the 726.60-carat stone was named in honor of the man who was then President of the country, Getúlio Vargas. The stone's discovery provides an example of how Harry Winston operated when the game was afoot. The jeweler flew to Brazil within a matter of hours after reading a brief newspaper item reporting the discovery. But when he landed in Rio, he found that the dealer had already sent it to Antwerp. Winston boarded the first ship he could get—one faster than that carrying the gem—and was in Antwerp before the diamond. He was the first to inspect it, and bought it immediately. Among the twenty-nine stones it yielded, seven emerald-cut diamonds totaling 176 carats were set in a bracelet in 1947 for a maharajah, who had them reset as a striking necklace five years later.

The Winston took its name from the jeweler himself, perhaps because he had fallen in love with the 62-carat flawless pear-shaped diamond. He told associates, "This stone is like a great painting. You want to keep on looking at it." In 1959 Winston sold the gem to the King of Saudi Arabia. A year and a half later, while concluding a $2 million sale of jewels to the King, Winston was given the diamond back, still inside its original wrappings. When Winston expressed amazement, the King explained: he had realized there was no way he could bestow one diamond among four wives, and that he would never have a moment's peace. Winston, who took back the stone, later found another that so closely matched it, he made a pair of earrings from the two and sold the jewels to a Canadian client. When the earrings were later auctioned in Geneva in 1981, they brought over $7 million.

COLORED JEWELS

The Catherine the Great emerald was a mere 61.49 carats (as compared with the sapphire of the same name, which was 337 carats) but had an interesting history. It had belonged to a woman who knew worthy jewels when she saw them, the Grand Duchess Vladimir, sister-in-law of Nicholas II, the last Tsar of Russia. The emerald was subsequently acquired by a Canadian industrialist who left it to his daughter, Melba McMartin Van Buren. It was from the Van Buren estate that Winston purchased it in 1948, mounting the stone as a ring that he gave on memorandum to King Farouk. The Egyptian monarch was forced to abdicate days after it arrived. Amazingly, he remembered to give the unpaid-for emerald to the American ambassador, asking him to return it to Winston. It was sold in 1953 to a Texan.

ZENDRINI

Carlo Ferrero Zendrini is an art collector. But the masterpieces he acquires to sell in his Rome, Turin, and Monte Carlo emporiums are not Leonardos; they are Art Deco jewels from the great French houses of Cartier, Boucheron, and Van Cleef & Arpels. Zendrini is the third generation to head a family business established by his grandmother, Amabile, in Turin in 1919. Under the direction of Carlo's mother, Carla Zendrini, the firm became known for antique jewelry and Continental silver that was eagerly sought by the Turinese aristocracy. In the 1950s Carla Zendrini began to buy Cartier pieces in Paris and London; but it was Carlo who, in the 1970s, began a serious study of the Cartier and Van Cleef archives that resulted in a collecting passion. Zendrini found that the extraordinary artistic designs from the 1920s and '30s interested him much more than the imposing jewels made for royalty and aristocrats of previous eras.

Zendrini's renowned collection, much of which has been acquired at auction, includes several legendary Cartier pieces, two of which were lent to the "Art of Cartier" exhibit at the Petit Palais in Paris for the bicentenary of the French Revolution. One, the Merle Oberon necklace, made for the actress in 1938, contains twenty-nine huge unfaceted emeralds, totaling 1,300 carats and hung from a diamond chain. The other is a "tutti-frutti" bracelet (colored stones carved as fruits and flowers) conceived in Paris in the 1920s for Mrs. Cole Porter at the time of Diaghilev's Ballets Russes. Zendrini donated this piece to the Cartier Museum in Geneva.

OPPOSITE, *cabochon emerald–and–diamond necklace commissioned from Cartier London in 1938 by Merle Oberon. A line*
of pavé-set diamond rondelles suspends twenty-nine graduated baroque emerald drops with diamond caps and diamond collet terminals.
Signed by Cartier, Paris; bought at auction by Carlo Zendrini.
Christie's New York

ABOVE, *necklace with three emerald drops, made in Paris by Chaumet, Place Vendôme, in the 1950s. Formerly in the collection of the Dupont de Nemours family.*
Zendrini Collection, Via Condotti, Roma

Jewel Thefts

*I*t is a salesperson's nightmare, a thief's dream: the switch, the con, the double cross, pulled off with perfect strategy, perfect timing. A second ago a diamond ring lay on the counter . . . now, it's gone. A hush falls over the jewelry salon as a quick inventory is taken, only to confirm that the ring is, indeed, missing. Did someone take it, and if so, who, how, when? As hearts race, anxiety gives way to dread. Yes, something was actually stolen right out from under the noses of security guards.

Theft is a hush-hush subject in the glamorous world of extraordinary jewels. To speak the word evokes fear of being jinxed or of compromising the security department, so jewelers are understandably reluctant to share their theft stories. They admit, though, that the subject is frequently brought up by customers, proving, perhaps, that theft stories—replete with drama, heroes, crooks, and blunders—always have appeal.

The common denominator in every jewel theft is, of course, greed coupled with the lust to hold something priceless and beautiful. Thieves don't discriminate as to a jewel's owner or origin. Royal jewels, important religious jewels, and stones new to the market are all potential targets. From the well-planned "heist" by pros to the impulsive "lift" by the incorrigible kleptomaniac, thefts occur continually, worldwide, in stores, homes, airports, and hotels. The smuggling of gemstones, particularly emeralds, from mine sites is also rampant. A report in *National Geographic* in 1990 estimated that 50 percent of the rough emeralds mined in Zambia are smuggled out by Senegalese who sell them in Switzerland.

Stolen pieces are usually broken up immediately and sold for the stones so that the jewels can never again be identified. Who knows, stolen stones may be glinting on your best friend's finger, or nesting in granny's jewelry box; and the owner will never know that they have been part of another jewel in times past.

Did the theft of a diamond necklace precipitate the French Revolution? Napoleon thought so, as have several historians. At least four books have been written about the scandalous affair that shook and possibly brought down the court of Louis XVI and his wife, Marie Antoinette. The story begins during the reign of Louis XV with the necklace itself, an extravagance of diamonds created by the Paris jewelers Boehmer and Bassenge. The jewel, as described by the nineteenth-century English historian Thomas Carlyle, contained "a row of seventeen glorious diamonds, as large almost as filberts," to which were fastened a festoon and pendants of diamonds, plus "a very Queen of Diamonds" on the bosom; then row upon row of tasseled stones that, when clasped, streamed down the back of the neck like the "Aurora Borealis."

Sapphire-and-diamond necklace centering upon a cushion-cut sapphire of 114.30 carats. (From the jewelry of Florence J. Gould)
Christie's New York

Necklace with graduated flowerhead clusters of cushion-shaped yellow sapphires and diamonds alternating with graduated cushion-shaped blue sapphires; a pear-shaped yellow sapphire-and-diamond floral drop is suspended by a small heart-shaped blue sapphire. Shown en suite with a ring, bracelet, and pair of ear pendants. Christie Images

Louis XV had certainly encouraged the jewelers to create the dazzling necklace as a gift for his mistress, Comtesse du Barry. But he died in 1774, leaving them to try and find another buyer. Louis XVI and Marie Antoinette refused it as too expensive—the price at the time was an astonishing Fr 90,000 (more than $2.5 million in today's money). The jewelers were desperate. They had gone into debt to buy the diamonds, had completed the necklace by 1778, and were using it as collateral for loans to stay in business.

In 1785 a court intriguer, Jeanne de Luz de Saint-Rémy de Valois, known as Comtesse de La Motte, was approached by the jewelers and asked to use her supposed influence to cajole the Queen into buying the necklace. Ambitious, seductive, and deceitful, La Motte had in fact created the impression that she enjoyed an intimate relationship with Marie Antoinette. She had also established a coterie of influential lovers that included Rétaux de Villette (the Queen's private secretary) and Cardinal de Rohan, the Grand Almoner of France. She immediately saw the possibility of a grand swindle, playing all the dupes off against each other to gain the necklace for herself.

La Motte enlisted Rétaux as the master forger, promising him a cut. Rétaux's letters, written on the Queen's own blue-bordered, gilt-edged stationery, indicated that she wished to buy the necklace without the King's knowledge. La Motte, using these letters, tricked the unsuspecting Cardinal de Rohan into acting as an intermediary. Rohan was, by the 1780s, out of favor with the Queen and leapt at the opportunity to be returned to her good graces.

Preying on Rohan's ambition—he aspired to be prime minister—La Motte arranged an absurd charade in the Versailles garden known as the Venus Grove. She enlisted a young prostitute who resembled Marie Antoinette to pose as the Queen. An evening rendezvous was staged in which the "Queen" handed Rohan a rose and murmured, "You know what this means."

Thoroughly convinced, Rohan signed a contract with the jewelers to buy the necklace on installments. The jewelers, thrilled with the prospect of the sale, gave the necklace to Rohan, who in turn handed it to a conspirator, who handed it to La Motte. Delighted with her success, La Motte proceeded to break up the necklace and buy herself furniture before sending the remainder of the stones to England to be sold. When Rohan was unable to pay the first installment in full, the jewelers went to the Queen, and thus the affair was exposed.

In 1785 Louis XVI had Cardinal de Rohan arrested and sent to the Bastille. The public viewed this as an arbitrary act of royal despotism, and the necklace—although never owned by Marie Antoinette—as the ultimate demonstration of the hated Queen's frivolity. Some people suspected that she had masterminded the affair in an effort to ruin the Cardinal. Rohan, though exonerated, was banished from court. La Motte was flogged, branded (with "V" for *voleuse, thief*), and imprisoned; but she escaped to England, where she proceeded to publish scandalous memoirs defaming Marie Antoinette, who was—most historians agree— guiltless in the affair of the necklace.

On the fateful evening of October 16, 1946, at Ednam Lodge, Sunningdale, England, while the servants were having tea, a burglar stole the Duchess of Windsor's black jewelry case from under her maid's bed. It contained about £25,000 in jewels, according to Scotland Yard, which never managed to solve the mysterious case. (Why, they wondered, did the Duke's dog not bark?) Although none of the jewels were ever recovered, the lucky Duke and Duchess recouped the full amount of the declared value from Lloyds of London, even though the jewels had not been stored in a safe as their insurance policy stipulated. With the windfall, the Duchess purchased the first of her Cartier panther jewels: a clip in the form of a snarling emerald-eyed, gold-and-enamel cat crouching on a cushion-shaped cabochon emerald of 90 carats.

The outcome of the crime, though fortuitous for the Windsors, fueled rumors, still bandied about, that the theft had been staged by the royal family in an attempt to recoup the vanished emeralds of Queen Alexandra. Some say the Duke had given them to the Duchess, who, ten years earlier, had appeared bedecked in emeralds at the opera. However, a list provided by the assessors of the jewels stolen at Ednam contained only one emerald, a ring of 7.81 carats. The so-called "Alexandra emeralds" have in fact never been definitively described or traced and remain as much of a mystery as the Ednam theft of the "Wallis collection."

Two sensational thefts occurred at the venerable headquarters of Tiffany & Co. in the 1950s, one by daring bandits, another by an adept female con artist. As recounted in *The Tiffany Touch* by Joseph Purtell:

> New York on that Sunday morning in August 1958 was quiet, as usual in midsummer. The downtown streets were empty. The only signs of activity were around St. Patrick's Cathedral, where worshipers were entering the church for the 6 o'clock mass. As the services began, a single car cruised up Fifth Avenue, past the cathedral, and continued on for six blocks, stopping in front of Tiffany's. A man got out, walked leisurely to the corner and glanced along Fifty-seventh Street. It, too, was without signs of life.
>
> The man went back to the car and lifted out a heavy sledgehammer; at the same moment a second man jumped from the car, carrying a second sledgehammer. They walked to the display windows, glittering with diamonds, which flank the Fifth Avenue entrance to the store, lifted the hammers and swung them in wide arcs. The heavy blows broke holes about five inches across in the centers of the windows of the five-eighth-inch-thick, supposedly shatterproof glass. The men thrust their arms through the holes and plucked out two diamond necklaces, a diamond pin and a diamond ring. Not more than a few minutes passed before they were back in the car and on their way up the avenue with $163,000 in jewelry.
>
> The armed guard and a detective inside the store heard nothing. Not until 6:15 A.M., when a patrolman walked by, was the incredibly bold robbery discovered, and the method reconstructed by the police. The robbers had been lucky, as well as meticulous, in timing their coup. The corner of Fifty-seventh Street and Fifth Avenue is what the police department terms a "post"; a patrolman is always kept there, since across from Tiffany's is a branch bank, and near another corner was Van Cleef and Arpels.
>
> But at 5:45 that particular Sunday morning, the officer had been sent to the Waldorf-Astoria to supplement the guard awaiting the arrival of Soviet Foreign Minister Andrei Gromyko, in the city to visit the United Nations. Ironically, the policeman was not needed; Gromyko had stopped off at the Russian embassy.

The daring robbery highlights the overall security problem which haunts stores like Tiffany's, which, as the press noted, "had been regarded as being as invulnerable as Fort Knox." The window smashing revealed a grave flaw in the security system; since no one had conceived of such a robbery the windows had not been wired into the central alarm system. After the fact, this was done, and the glass replaced with panes which were proved to be shatterproof in the best possible test. A second robbery attempt was made several months later, this time by firing two bullets into the windows, but the only damage was two small holes on a corner.

The jewelry taken in the first instance was never recovered. Nevertheless, Tiffany's did not change its policy and follow the practice of most important jewelers who replace displays at night with inexpensive articles or artificial stones. Windows with phony diamonds would not be genuine Tiffany windows.

Chairman Hoving felt the same as a long-time customer who said, "After all, when do couples go strolling along the avenue on a window-shopping spree? At night and on Sundays. Where do they pause? At Tiffany's. And where do they return next day to buy a part of the dream? Tiffany's."

Tiffany's also has had its share of loss through trickery. One of the most successful frauds was engineered at the end of the last century by a "lady Detroiter," as Jack Manning, a civically proud Detroit columnist, has recalled. This was Sophie Lyons, who achieved global notoriety during the eighties and nineties, abetted by her devoted husband, Billie Burke. Sophie, who reformed and devoted her time to "rehabilitating criminals, especially youthful ones," told a police official about the time she took Tiffany's.

As the columnist wrote:

> Sophie swept regally into the store and demanded to be shown an assortment of rubies and diamonds. She was a superb actress and could dress and talk like a patrician. She examined this stone and that and finally announced there was nothing suitable and rose to leave. Then the clerk noticed to his chagrin that seven expensive stones were missing, worth about fifty grand. She and the clerk were the only persons within touching distance. Was it possible she had dropped them into her handbag? The lady drew herself up in haughty indignation. The clerk called a store detective . . . and she was escorted into a room and searched by a matron. Nary a stone was found on her, and she threw the place into an uproar, threatening damages for humiliation, false arrest, etc. . . . eventually, she exited, the management apologizing. As Sophie said, "the most sullen and baffled apology you can imagine. They were not stupid. They knew I had taken the stones but they were helpless." . . . The next day her husband strolled nonchalantly into Tiffany's, bought a diamond ring from the same clerk his wife had tricked, and paid cash. While the clerk was making out the receipt, Billie slipped the seven stolen gems from the gum under the counter where Sophie had stuck them and walked out a happier and wealthier man.

The trick of the beautiful blonde in 1950 was quite as ingenious. She examined a tray of engagement rings and finally narrowed her preference to two, one for $2,550 and one for $3,250. She finally said she couldn't make up her mind; could she please show the rings to her mother who was sick in a nearby hotel? Naturally, the salesman could come along. The salesman did, and also a detective. Would they mind waiting in the sitting room of the suite while the customer went in to her mother in the bedroom. Always gentlemen, the Tiffany men sat down to wait. They waited, and waited, and waited. The same idea occurred to both at the same time. They ran into the bedroom. It was empty—an open door leading into the hall showed where the blonde and the rings had gone.

The most audacious trick of all was performed by another woman, again described as "a perfect lady." She pulled off her remarkable coup in 1965, under the eyes of closely watching detectives and salesmen. What is more, she was able to defraud both Tiffany's and Harry Winston's in the space of fifteen minutes. The razzle-dazzle started at Tiffany's. As she approached the diamond counter, the clerk noticed she was wearing an expensive marquise diamond ring. She asked to see something in higher-priced marquise rings. Impressed by the customer's gem, the salesman brought out several rings, leaving them on the counter while the lady tried on first one and then another, comparing the stones. Eventually, she said she simply could not make up her mind and left the store.

She walked down a block to Harry Winston's and asked to see their more expensive rings, laying her own ring on a table. Again, the suitably impressed salesman brought out a number of marquise rings. Nevertheless, since the customer was not known, she was more closely watched than usual by a security guard, an ex-FBI man. Eventually, as she had at Tiffany's, the woman said she could not make up her mind and left the store. It was not until later, when they checked over their stock and talked to each other, that the salesmen at Tiffany's and Winston's learned what had happened.

At Tiffany's the "perfect lady" had exchanged the 2.75-carat diamond worth $7,500 that she had worn into the store for one weighing 3.69 carats, worth $19,800, which she wore going out. She walked into Winston's wearing the Tiffany ring, and with two men closely watching, managed to exchange it for a Winston ring of 5.30 carats, worth $38,500. The daring and nerve of the woman who had tricked the two most closely guarded stores in the country aroused the grudging admiration even of Winston. "She was not a professional thief," he said, "just a woman who wanted a more expensive ring to wear." As might be expected the slick switch brought another new rule at Tiffany's: never more than two rings on the counter at the same time.

Diane Dillon, Seaman Schepps's granddaughter, was in the Park Avenue shop one day in the late 1980s when a man came in claiming to be picking up a package for a customer. He was dressed as a messenger except for the Uzi machine gun he was carrying. The rather unsubtle thief motioned to Dillon to empty the safe; she then added everything from petty cash, the cash drawers, and her own handbag. All the while,

Rivière-style diamond necklace composed of thirty graduated brilliant-cut diamonds weighing a total of 192.96 carats; and a ring with a brilliant-cut 12.76-carat diamond set between tapered baguette-cut diamond shoulders.
Christie Images

a wealthy customer who Dillon recalls was "dripping in diamonds" browsed oblivious to the theft taking place in the tiny shop. The entire incident was over in about six minutes, and the thief fled in a car, absconding with more cash than jewelry. Dillon believes he was probably stuck in traffic in the same block the whole time she was giving the police a report. The customer, who had seen the car, was no help.

Humphrey Butler of Christie's London office was present at a daring robbery that occurred as the result of an error published by the auction house's PR department. In 1984 an exhibition of Florence Gould's jewels was scheduled to run for three days; but a fourth day was advertised by mistake on a stunning poster that carried a picture of the important sapphire-and-diamond necklace that was to be featured in the sale, so Christie's decided to honor the error. During the morning session of the additional day—reserved for members of the trade—four unmasked, and apparently unarmed, men walked quietly up the staircase. But halfway up, they pulled on masks and drew sawed-off shotguns. Three of the robbers held people at gunpoint in the reception area, forcing them to lie on the floor, while the fourth used a sledgehammer to smash the cases containing the Gould pieces and other important items. Shouting to add to the confusion, in just thirteen seconds (as recorded by the security video cameras) the thieves grabbed a bracelet, a single earring, and an important diamond necklace—about two million dollars' worth of jewelry.

A young woman trainee from Phillips, a rival auction house, had been viewing the Gould necklace with Butler, and during the commotion she shoved the jewel toward him at his signal. He slipped it into his pocket. Neither stolen jewels nor thieves were ever found, despite the offer of a large reward. "It was a proverbial 'smash and grab,' " said Butler. But thanks to his quick thinking, the magnificent sapphire "poster" necklace was saved.

In September 1989, *The Wall Street Journal* reported the mysterious and traumatic ordeal that began at the airport in Palm Beach for Felice Lippert, co-founder of Weight Watchers International. On her way to New York, where she planned to attend several parties, Lippert had put jewelry valued at nearly half a million dollars into her Vuitton handbag. She dutifully placed the bag on the X-ray machine's conveyor belt . . . and never saw it again! At first, she thought that someone might have mistakenly taken her bag, but she was unable to persuade airport security or Delta Airlines to help her find it. The jewels it contained were ones she had collected on trips around the world, all uninsured except for a $75,000 pair of diamond earrings purchased from Van Cleef & Arpels. But as the evidence had vanished, who would believe her? Although Lippert filed suit against the airline and the firm that operated the security gate, she could not prove that her bag contained the jewels she described. Months later, Véronique Ma'arop of Van Cleef & Arpels was perusing a Sotheby's catalog for an upcoming sale and recognized Lippert's earrings—despite the fact that the central diamonds had been replaced with rubies. She was able to vouch for Lippert and retrieve the earrings, although Sotheby's would not identify the consignor. Lippert's evidence convinced a jury to rule for her reimbursement in the amount of $431,000; but in 1993 the Florida Supreme Court overruled the decision, allowing her only $1,250, which is the limit for lost luggage.

It was the glittering French Riviera, Antibes on the Côte d'Azur to be exact, where villas, yachts, and Bentleys are the norm. It was the glamorous setting for Alfred Hitchcock's 1955 thriller *To Catch a Thief;* but in the summer of 1993, real-life players outdazzled Hollywood with their wealth and daring in what was certainly one of the major jewel thefts of the century.

Denver billionaire oilman Marvin Davis (chairman and chief executive of Paramount Communications) and his wife, Barbara, had arrived at Nice airport in their private jet, a Boeing 727. Switching to a gold-colored chauffered Cadillac limousine, they headed for the exclusive Hôtel du Cap, one of the very few luxury hotels that accept neither checks nor credit cards. So all guests, as is well known, arrive with hefty bankrolls. The flamboyant Davises, among the world's biggest spenders, were no exception. (Barbara Davis is famous not only for her spectacular jewelry, but also for having her dresses made—by Nolan Miller—to match.) The couple had $10,000,000 in jewels and $50,000 in cash packed in the truck of the limo, which wended its way to the hotel along the serpentine Boulevard du Cap.

All at once, a Renault darted in front of the limo and blocked its path while another car drove up behind it. Four hooded gunmen jumped out, held machine guns to the chauffeur's and the Davises' heads, and indicated, without words, that the chauffeur was to open the trunk. The gunmen seized the jewels and cash, and snatched at a necklace valued at $40,000 around Barbara's neck. They couldn't make the clasp work, and since they spoke no English, they finally broke the necklace—nearly breaking Barbara's neck as well. Then they fled. The terrifying theft, which Davis suspected was an inside job ("They knew our every move"), took about two minutes.

None of the jewelry was ever recovered except a 32-carat diamond ring, which the thieves had apparently dropped and which was found, appropriately enough, under a rock.

At 95.40 carats, the emerald-cut Golconda d'Or is one of the largest golden diamonds ever mined. Its checkered history (recounted in more detail in the "Introduction") mentions its disappearance from the Turkish crown jewels in the nineteenth century. In 1960 the magnificent stone was purchased at auction by the Melbourne jewelry firm Dunklings, which in 1978 was taken over by another firm, Angus & Coote, which exhibited the stone to raise money for charity.

For a benefit at the Sydney Town Hall, the Golconda d'Or was mounted in an elevated display case, requiring that the stone be inserted from below through a padlocked door. The exhibition lasted a full week, giving the robbers—a ring of tough international criminals—plenty of time to plan their daring heist. The display case was illuminated from above by a light fixture that, as it turned out, was not securely fastened.

The thieves struck in broad daylight, with crowds of people milling about admiring the various displays— antique cars, old books, et cetera. A woman came in carrying two gift-wrapped boxes, each about a foot square. These were in fact stepping stones to get to the jewel. She put them down right next to the Golconda display case, then distracted a guard while her accomplice, a man, stacked the boxes on top of each other, climbed up, and easily removed the light fixture from the top of the case. This created a hole large enough for his hand, with which he took the Golconda d'Or and replaced it with a fake. Tony Coote of Angus & Coote recalled that the thief was so cool that when an elderly lady asked him what he was doing, he replied, "Just replacing the diamond." By the time the woman's screams alerted a guard, the thieves, and the priceless Golconda d'Or, had vanished. Although Interpol was summoned and conducted searches of all ports in Australia, the stone was never recovered.

On January 20, 1977, a salesperson at Bulgari's shop in New York's Hotel Pierre received a call from a gentleman who said he was a guest at the hotel and wondered if jewelry could be brought to the room for viewing. This was not an uncommon request and simply required that basic security procedures be followed. After a call to the front desk confirmed that the man was indeed registered at the hotel, the salesperson, accompanied by a security guard, took some pieces up to the man's room. A second and third trip followed, with different selections. Each time, the scene in the room was chaotic, as a different person—manicurist, tailor, barber—would be tending to the man's needs. At one point the man announced that he felt ill and asked everybody to leave the room immediately. When the Bulgari salesperson returned to the shop, he discovered that a double emerald-cut diamond ring set in platinum, and valued at $40,000, was missing. A call to the room confirmed suspicions that the "guest" had already checked out.

A month later the FBI called Bulgari to say that they had located the thief, incarcerated in Michigan. He was a known con artist with a long criminal record. He had died while in jail, and in accordance with the law, an autopsy had been performed at once. Much to the astonishment of the prison authorities, a diamond ring matching the description of the Bulgari piece was found in the man's stomach. A Bulgari representative flew to Michigan, where he verified and claimed the ring. As for the crook, no one will ever know when he swallowed the evidence, why it had not passed through his system, and if, in ingesting it, he had in fact hastened his own demise.

Often the witness to, or victim of, a theft gives in to an ill-advised knee-jerk reaction either to chase the thief or to try to outwit him. In hindsight, these same people usually deplore their own reckless behavior. Take Charles Dishman, who, while president of C. D. Peacock in Chicago, saw a man steal a Patek Phillippe watch using a fake-bottom box. Dishman ran after the thief, chasing him into and through the subway until the robber jumped through a plate-glass window at Marshall Field. "That's when I stopped chasing him," said Dishman, who later realized that he might easily have been shot.

Another jewelry executive who survived his own poor judgment recalls a potentially deadly stickup at a posh New York restaurant. A gunman jumped up on the bar and demanded that the patrons put all their jewelry, credit cards, and cash in the centers of the tables. He threatened to kill anyone he caught holding back. As the robber made his way around the room, the executive could not bring himself to surrender his very expensive gold Rolex and hid it under a crumpled napkin, where, miraculously, it remained unnoticed. After the gunman had fled with everything else, the man recognized his recklessness as virtually suicidal behavior and was so upset he was never able to wear the watch again. He gave it to his brother.

Some robbers are just plain dumb and forget to do their homework. There's many a tale, for example, of thieves who hold up stores unaware that the merchandise is virtually worthless imitation jewelry. Other benighted crooks attempt thefts in private showing rooms, unaware that security cameras are recording their every move. In one such instance, a kleptomaniac socialite made a habit of surreptitiously stuffing jewels into her girdle until the store manager told her husband that he would be charged for any items that did not come out of the showing room. Another naive thief attempted to steal a diamond ring by inserting it into one of his bodily orifices, an outrageous act witnessed by the security people, who were watching him on the video monitor. When confronted, he denied all until threatened with a nurse, who, it was explained, would retrieve the ring with surgical tools.

LEFT, *Duke and Duchess of Windsor, 1943.*
Bettmann Newsphotos

RIGHT, *Elizabeth Taylor.*
A. Tannenbaum/SYGMA

Some of the most interesting stories come from jewelry expert Lincoln Foster, formerly of De Beers Consolidated Mines Ltd. and former senior vice president of Tiffany & Co. Now an antiques dealer in Virginia, Foster recalls two clever attempts to beat the system at the source—the great diamond mines of South Africa.

Kleinzee, an alluvial mine located in the remote desert region of Namaqualand, was the setting for one such story. Workers left the site only ten times a year and each time were X-rayed. The only private vehicle allowed to come and go on the premises belonged to the general manager; the rest were Land Rovers restricted to the mining property. One mechanic cleared to work on the manager's car collected diamonds over a period of time and stashed them in the car's gas tank. When the manager left on vacation, the mechanic took his leave at the same time, followed the manager, stole the car, sliced open the gas tank, and retrieved several pounds of diamonds. But when the manager took his car in to have the gas tank repaired, a few stray diamonds were found, giving authorities enough of a clue so that the crook was eventually caught and many of the diamonds recovered.

A clever nurse at Kleinzee devised an equally ingenious scheme. Once, when medical supplies had to be transported, she hid uncut diamonds in bottles of penicillin. Later, she tried to sell them to a cutter in Johannesburg—unaware that a permit was needed to sell uncut stones. The diamond cutter alerted the authorities and she was caught.

So why would a person risk everything just to steal a stone or jewel? Clearly, it is a combination of factors: the beauty, value, and timeless allure of gemstones; their convenient portability; and the ease with which they can be traded and converted into new, untraceable jewels. All conspire to keep jewelry theft flourishing as one of mankind's oldest professions, popular with royalty and commoner in equal measure.

Auctions

*I*nspiration for this book came in large measure from the great auction houses, Sotheby's and Christie's, which have in recent years emerged as important promoters and marketers of extraordinary jewels. The expanded role of auctions in jewelry sales is a phenomenon of the affluent 1980s, when a remarkable number of private individuals—as opposed to members of the jewelry trade—acquired the degree of wealth necessary to purchase the world's most precious adornments. This success has continued into the 1990s, and it is the increased presence of the private buyer that has led the auction houses to upgrade their catalogues by means of excellent color photography and—perhaps even more important—technical and historical documentation and presale estimates. In the past, as recently as the 1970s, a signed piece was not necessarily noted as such; but today one can expect to find extensive and informative captions: for example, a biographical note on a designer or a brief essay on a jewelry house. In addition, significant stones are sure to be accompanied by grading certificates from the GIA (Gemological Institute of America).

In auction parlance, jewels of the highest quality and value are termed "Magnificent." Jewels of somewhat lesser value are classified accordingly as "Highly Important" and "Fine." Many well-established auction houses, such as Phillips, Butterfield, and Weschler's in America, routinely offer noteworthy sales of jewels in the latter categories, including "Antique" (which connotes the nineteenth century and earlier).

The auction is an international marketplace for jewels, with the most important sales occurring in New York, London, Geneva, St. Moritz, and other European capitals. As Christie's jewelry director, François Curiel, has commented, "The auction has become the thermostat of the jewelry market." Through subscriptions to catalogues, prospective buyers can review these sales in advance. Thus, the need to travel around the world to see the best jewelry collections has been eliminated. Today one can sit in Idaho and bid via telephone on a jewel being offered in Geneva. That's progress.

There are, of course, a limited number of truly significant gems, and serious private buyers and dealers are aware of them as they go in and out of collections. The rival auction houses compete fiercely to obtain magnificent gems and jewels for their sales. When the quality of the merchandise matches the provenance (record of previous ownership) of the consignor, as in the 1987 sale of the Duchess of Windsor's jewels, the result is often a promotional windfall, as Sotheby's John Block describes in the pages that follow.

To bid competitively and intelligently at auction, one must do one's homework—actually see and carefully examine the merchandise, either in person or through a proxy. In every auction catalogue, no matter how exquisite the merchandise, there is the warning that lots are sold "as is" and thus must be scrutinized for damage, resettings, substitutions, and so forth. Prospective buyers may bring appraisers and gem experts to presale exhibitions. A jewelry expert employed by an auction house can be relied upon not just to romance the stones but to provide guidance, both to items in and to procedures of a particular sale. Dealers armed with specialized knowledge of the gem trade have the edge at an auction, but knowledgeable private collectors are ever more in evidence.

Many of the beautiful photographs in this book were supplied by Sotheby's and Christie's. I am indeed grateful to the representatives of these distinguished houses for their cooperation. Their statements follow.

CHRISTIE'S

by François Curiel
International Director of Jewelry

*T*oday more jewelry is changing hands in the auction salerooms than at any other time in history. In the first year of this decade, we estimate that the major auction houses sold $370 million in jewelry. The sheer volume and quality are ample evidence that auction houses now play a vital role in the jewelry industry worldwide. Although this phenomenal increase in sales began only twenty years ago, there have been jewelry auctions since the late eighteenth century.

James Christie, who founded the house that bears his name, held his first major jewelry sale in London in 1795, when the jewels of Madame du Barry became available following her trial and 1793 execution. The sale was described in the catalogue as "a Most Capital and Superb Assemblage of Valuable Jewels of Most Singular Excellence, Beauty and Perfection, late the property of Madame La Comtesse du Barry, deceased." The jewels brought just under £10,000, the equivalent of $2 million today.

In the nineteenth century, collections of increasing importance began to pass through Christie's salerooms: the Marlborough gems, a vast collection of cameos and intaglios, were sold in 1873. A few years later the jewels of Lily, Duchess of Marlborough, were sold. A major sale of the twentieth century was that of the Russian imperial jewels in 1927, dispersed when the Soviets were in urgent need of hard currency.

Since then, jewelry has represented a significant share of Christie's business, and the company has become a major source for magnificent jewels, claiming 39 percent of the world market. The term *market* in this instance embraces Christie's, Sotheby's, and several American houses, in addition to the Hôtel Drouot in Paris and a few other European houses.

In recent years the collections of Florence J. Gould, Ailsa Mellon Bruce, and Caroline Ryan Foulke have been sold at Christie's with impressive results. The list of celebrated persons whose jewelry has come under the Christie's hammer reads like an international Who's Who: Nelson Rockefeller, Joan Crawford, Merle Oberon, Mary Pickford, Cecil B. DeMille, Ingrid Bergman, Dame Margot Fonteyn, Mrs. Armand Hammer, Majorie Merriweather Post, Anna Case Mackay, to name a few.

In 1968 Christie's opened an office in Geneva, the first outside the United Kingdom. In its first ten years this office sold more than $310 million in jewelry alone.

In May 1976 the company expanded further, opening a New York office on Park Avenue and, two years later, a secondary saleroom, Christie's East. Today Christie's maintains thirteen offices in the United States and additional offices in a total of thirty-one countries, as well as sales centers in nine countries.

Four times a year, twice in Geneva and twice in New York, the major auction houses hold sales that provide the jewelry trade with a forum in which to assemble, buy and sell, and generally take the pulse of the market.

The sometimes staggering prices realized for jewelry at auction give credibility to retail prices. If, for example, a private collector is hesitant to pay a million dollars for a Kashmir sapphire in a shop, sales resistance is lessened when a similar auction price can be demonstrated. This sort of validation illustrates how auction houses and the international jewelry trade depend upon each other. In fact, the active participation of the trade is crucial to the success of major auction sales. While private collectors may often be able to pay higher prices, they are unlikely to attend every sale, examine every item, mark every lot in the catalogue—routine procedure in the trade. Christie's and the other auction houses—whether they care to admit it or not—welcome the average ratio of 60 percent private buyers to 40 percent trade at their sales.

It is important for the private buyer to observe the trade's involvement in sales. A recent case in point was the purchase by a private collector of an invisibly set ruby-and-diamond flower brooch by Van Cleef & Arpels for $400,000. The underbidder was Jacques Arpels himself. This distinguished jeweler, a legend in the industry, recognized the importance of keeping auction prices at a certain level to demonstrate to the public that a signed Van Cleef & Arpels jewel will not be sold for less at auction than in a Van Cleef & Arpels salon. In a similar way, Eric Nussbaum, the director of the Cartier Museum, in Geneva, frequently bids on behalf of the house of Cartier for jewels and objects produced by this world-famous company.

These days a record price is set at almost every auction but is valid only until the next sale. Records are usually realized for large historic single stones or signed jewels of impeccable provenance. Many world-record prices have been realized at Christie's, among them the highest auction price per carat for a colored diamond, for a colorless diamond, and for a gray diamond. The colored diamond, a very rare fancy purplish-red circular-cut stone weighing only .95 carats, sold for $880,000, or $926,315 per carat. By comparison, the colorless D flawless diamond of 52.59 carats sold for $7,480,000, or $142,232 per carat. The enormous discrepancy in per-carat prices demonstrates the extreme rarity of red diamonds.

We have also realized record prices for single natural pearls, for a single lot of jade, for an Art Nouveau jewel, for an opal, and for an invisibly set bracelet.

Many factors contribute to value, including rarity, condition, design, importance of maker's signature, and provenance. But it is, above all, the intrinsic value of the stones that ultimately determines the auction price and, not incidentally, stimulates interest in the market.

Jewelry comes into the auction market on consignment from owners who, with the auction experts, agree upon a reserve price: the amount below which the item will not be sold. The reserve must be realistic enough to ensure a satisfactory sale while minimizing the risk of "buy-in," the auction term for no sale. Jewelry consigned in one location may be sold in another where comparable items are being offered—and where the auction house determines that the highest price will be realized. A consigned item is placed in the next scheduled sale so the least possible time is lost in the completion of the transaction.

Different types of jewels are sold in different venues. London is the center for antique jewelry; New York specializes in signed jewelry of great intrinsic value; and Hong Kong sees much interest in jade. Geneva remains the major international venue thanks to lenient import tax regulations and the ne plus ultra confidentiality of the Swiss banking system. Today, the highest prices for important jewelry are achieved in Geneva, New York, and London.

Sales are scheduled regularly, with time allowed for the preparation of comprehensive catalogues, and for promotion and publicity in order to give potential buyers time to plan to attend. For days—in some cases weeks or months—before a sale, jewelry is exhibited, sometimes in several venues. At these previews, private collectors may call upon outside experts, such as gemologists and jewelry historians, to examine the jewels and to substantiate the opinions of the auction specialists.

Christie's publishes some of the most accurate and luxuriously illustrated catalogues in the auction field. We are proud of having introduced notes, references, and biographies of owners and makers, which turned once ordinary sales brochures into historical documents. Like all auction houses, we maintain extensive mailing lists of catalogue subscribers who rely on these important catalogues as essential to major sales.

There are two major advantages of selling and buying at auction: the speed with which entire estates can be dispersed—literally at the tap of a gavel; and the tremendous range of extraordinary jewelry, far broader than could be offered in any but the largest retail establishments.

Buyers may bid in a variety of ways, most usually in person by raising a numbered paddle. Telephone bids are taken for those who cannot attend a sale in person, and surprisingly, perhaps, many of the largest sales are concluded this way. In New York in 1991, for example, a Cartier Egyptian Revival Temple Gate clock was "knocked down" to a telephone bidder for $1,540,000, a record for an Art Deco clock. There are also order bids, given in writing to the auctioneer, who executes them for the bidder. All bids are equally important and satisfactory to the house and buyer, respectively.

I am often asked to describe the typical jewelry auction buyer. Apart from the obvious—financial ability to purchase costly objects—what all seem to share is the heart of a passionate collector who longs for beauty and appreciates craftsmanship. Usually it is older collectors who are selling and younger collectors, having achieved financial independence, who are buying. Private collectors look for jewels to wear and enjoy while turning a prudent eye toward the possibility of eventual resale. Dealers sometimes buy for break-up purposes if the value of the stones exceeds the piece's historic, stylistic, or esthetic importance.

Competition among the great auction houses is keen—often heated—especially so in the jewelry field. In the quest to obtain the choicest items for sale, we often spend months negotiating with estate attorneys and talking with clients, who for a variety of reasons must part with family treasures. Consignors must be handled with delicacy, tact, and understanding and with an eye to marketing strategies. A consignment contract is often the result of finely honed public relations skills and an ability to negotiate successfully. Finally, we must muster the patience to wait and see what will happen.

Some major jewelry items or collections require months or years to acquire; others simply walk in the door unexpectedly with their owners. As world records are set, the sales results become breakfast table conversation and newspaper headlines around the world.

The jewelry market is dynamic. There is always action. Rumors are rife and auction houses, dealers, and collectors are constantly jockeying for position. Excitement always intensifies as the sale date approaches.

Christie's, with its distinguished past clearly in view, now looks forward with enthusiasm and optimism to the future. The supply of beautiful gems and jewelry is unlikely to run out, and the auction saleroom will continue to fulfill its role as long as humankind honors one of its most primary instincts: to decorate the body and to possess what is the most concentrated and portable form of wealth to be found on the planet.

SOTHEBY'S

by John D. Block
Senior Vice President
Director of the Jewelry and Precious Objects Division
Sotheby's New York

*S*otheby's was founded in 1744 in London by a bookseller named Samuel Baker in order to bring together buyers and sellers of private libraries. When Baker died in 1778, his nephew John Sotheby broadened the firm's base to include the public sale of fine furniture, porcelain, antiquities, and jewelry. In the subsequent two and a half centuries, Sotheby's became one of the world's leading auction houses, with auction sales for 1991 of over $1.1 billion. In 1964 Sotheby's established itself in New York with the acquisition of Parke-Bernet Galleries on Madison Avenue. London, Geneva, and New York were the sites of the firm's major jewelry auctions until the late 1980s. But in 1988, with jewelry sales at Sotheby's New York surpassing $102 million, the international center for jewelry sales was firmly established there.

Sotheby's jewelry division has handled many famous collections dispersed to many famous collectors. The owners of important jewelry collections are often very glamorous people. The Duchess of Windsor, Daisy Fellowes, Annie Laurie Aiken, Countess Mona Bismarck, Clare Boothe Luce, Andy Warhol, Mrs. Harry Winston, and Marlene Dietrich have all added their own mystique to the gems they possessed. The value of the jewelry is enriched by its wealth of fabled associations. A great many of the jewels that come to Sotheby's for auction bring with them a heady mix of history, romance, and headlines, so that the sales acquire the atmosphere of movie premieres or museum openings.

One jewelry auction that captured the public's imagination occurred in May 1968, when Richard Burton acquired the famous Krupp diamond for Elizabeth Taylor for the then diamond auction record of $305,000. The excitement of this sale was surpassed the following year when Burton's agent vied with representatives of Cartier for a 69.4-carat diamond drop. The bidding war for the gem, which had been cut by Harry Winston and had a superb gemological rating, was described by an observer as "one of the most electrifying in auction history." Cartier's winning bid of $1,050,000 was a world record price for any piece of jewelry. Burton subsequently bought the stone directly from Cartier for somewhat more, and the stone was named the Taylor-Burton diamond.

In the late 1970s, inflation made fine gems and jewelry attractive to speculators, who began to buy stones for their investment value alone and stored them in bank vaults along with stocks and bonds. Auction prices rose dramatically. For example, the price for 1-carat D flawless diamonds reached a height of $50,000 to $60,000 per carat. In 1980 the speculative auction market peaked with the sale at Sotheby's Geneva of a pair of pear-shaped D-color diamond pendant earrings, weighing a total of 120 carats, for $6,650,000.

Then in 1981 the economic recession caused the bottom to fall out of the auction market, affecting both dealers, who ceased buying, and sellers, who withheld goods from the auction market. But the depressed economy enabled auction houses to reassess the jewelry market and develop strategies to attract new buyers and sellers. Sotheby's recognized the importance of the catalogue as the primary selling tool and decided to reproduce the jewels in full-color photographs instead of black-and-white, as had been traditional. We also recognized the importance of impeccable scholarship, so that excellent color photographs were augmented with full descriptive captions, historical anecdotes, and gemological references—enabling purchasers to confidently assess the stones and jewelry in upcoming sales.

Sotheby's also expanded its public relations and marketing activities in the 1980s to include special events, publications, brochures, newsletters, and private and public exhibitions. Our commitment to reach all possible buyers resulted in landmark sales during that decade.

In 1986 the sale of the jewels of the late Annie Laurie Aiken, a famous sportswoman and hostess, and mother of Sunny Von Bulow, realized half a million dollars more than the highest estimates. The success of that and other estate sales suggested that executors believed selling at auction in an open and competitive manner would enable heirs to achieve the highest possible prices.

But the most publicized estate auction in modern times, and one that exceeded *all* expectations, occurred in April 1987 with the sale of the jewels of the Duchess of Windsor to benefit the Pasteur Institute's AIDS research. In promoting this sale, Sotheby's launched an unprecedented worldwide effort. We published an elegant hardcover catalogue that includes striking color photographs of the Duchess's jewels, together with classic black-and-white photographs of the Duke and Duchess taken during their courtship and throughout their marriage by Cecil Beaton, Horst, Patrick Lichfield, and Karsh of Ottawa.

Since virtually every stage of the couple's relationship was marked by a gift of jewelry, often inscribed in a facsimile of the Duke's handwriting with "WE" (for Wallis and Edward) and a romantic sentiment, the catalogue's text supplemented descriptions of the jewels with explanations of the inscriptions and excerpts from the couple's love letters, diaries, and reminiscences.

The result was both the story of the couple's private romantic history and a guide to classic jewelry designs of the 1930s, '40s, and '50s. Some of the most spectacular items in the sale were the Cartier panther jewels designed by Jeanne Toussaint. The Duke was so proprietary about the jewels he helped design for the Duchess that in his will he expressed the desire that the pieces be broken up so that no other woman would ever be able to wear them.

To heighten interest in the sale and for security reasons, a presale exhibition tour of the Windsor jewels was limited to New York, Palm Beach, and Geneva, where the sale was to be held. A major publicity campaign capitalized on the mixture of royal scandal, legendary romance, fascinating jewelry, and high society that had always characterized the "love story of the century." By the time the jewels reached Sotheby's New York in March, the four-day public exhibition assumed the dimensions of a blockbuster art exhibit.

People waited for hours in long lines to see the Duchess's emerald engagement ring, her signature flamingo brooch, her diamond charm bracelet hung with nine gold jewel-encrusted crosses, and her collection of Cartier "great cat" jewels.

As the sale dates approached, price estimates were revised upward as Sotheby's predicted that perhaps twice the $10 million market value of the collection would be realized. But in fact, pieces in the sale went for ten to fifty times the estimate. The McLean/Windsor diamond, estimated at $968,000, went for $3,153,302 to a Japanese jeweler and businessman. The Cartier onyx-and-diamond panther bracelet, estimated at $225,800, went for $1,393,320. (It was rumored that the Princess of Wales had her heart set on this piece but that the Queen refused to have such a vibrant reminder of the Duchess of Windsor worn on the arm of a member of the royal family.)

A small white enameled photograph frame mounted with semiprecious colored stones that had a high estimate of $520 was sold for $403,329; and the Duchess's emerald-and-diamond engagement ring, with the original mount inscribed "We are ours now," which was estimated at $516,200, was sold for $2,126,646, which incidentally became the highest auction price ever paid for a single emerald.

Elizabeth Taylor bought the Prince of Wales brooch for $623,000, bidding from her poolside in California. The diamond clip designed as the plumes and crown of the Prince of Wales had, she said, special associations for her because she and Richard Burton were friends of the Windsors and she had always loved it as a jewel and he had loved it because of its Welsh origin.

Overall, the sale realized $50 million, a world record many times over. The ramifications of this sale were immediate and far-reaching, and the "Windsor fallout" continues to influence the market today, not least in a resurgence of interest in Cartier panther jewels, and even in *faux* jewels that replicate classics like the flamingo clip, by now a symbol of the Duchess's collection.

In the past, auction houses relied on the three D's—death, divorce, and debt—to bring sellers to the market; in the 1980s we discovered that we could also sell new jewels and gems as well. In response to clients' demands, we included newly manufactured jewels, diamonds from cutters, and cultured pearls from the farms. The vitality of the market for superb stones—without history or provenance—was demonstrated in

1986 when a 32.47-carat D flawless pear-shaped diamond was sold for $1,760,000, at the time a record for any jewel sold in an American auction. In 1990, when a 101.84-carat D flawless diamond realized $12,760,000, a new record was set for any jewel at auction. It was a fitting end to a decade that saw the auction business revolutionized by new marketing techniques and an influx of increasingly appreciative and sophisticated buyers.

Sotheby's holds four major jewelry auctions a year, in October, December, April, and June. They are planned to include great antique and period pieces, important diamonds and colored stones, and select pieces of estate jewelry. Each auction offers both a variety of stones and a range in prices.

It is the aim of the auction business to develop long-term relationships. We often appraise jewels that will not come to auction for fifty years. We repair jewelry and work with clients to upgrade their collections, even offering advice on buying at retail when an item does not come up for auction. Our goal is to make sure that people who want beautiful jewelry get good value.

It is exciting for buyers when wonderful jewels come on the market, and gratifying to buyers and sellers alike when jewels realize their worth in public sale. The nature of this transition is beautifully summarized by Albina du Boisrouvray, daughter of Luz Mila Patino and Count Guy du Boisrouvray, in the Preface she wrote to the catalogue of Sotheby's sale of her parents' magnificent jewels, which realized $30 million in 1989. She wrote: "I feel that these rare and precious belongings must circulate, get on with their lives, find new families. . . . I very much hope that the new owners of these various pieces will enjoy them immensely and will take as good and loving care of them as did three generations of our family and that the new owners of these objects, so dear to our hearts, will find through and with them great satisfaction."

The Animal Kingdom

*S*chlumberger and Claflin for Tiffany & Co., Cartier, Verdura, David Webb, Van Cleef & Arpels, Graff, and Boivin are a few of the major names associated with whimsical animal jewelry. Animals, from Africa to one's own backyard, play a significant part in this glamorous kingdom. Bears, panthers, elephants, koalas, mice, and lizards have been transformed into works of artful adornment and can be seen with emerald, ruby, or sapphire eyes and elaborate, colorful bodies. Animal themes in jewelry also come from the sea and air, and include starfish, mollusk shells, frogs, dragonflies, birds, and butterflies.

Many of the jewelry animals look as if they had just popped out of a favorite storybook, while others are rendered with a degree of realism. Some, like the little mouse designed by Fulco di Verdura, have even been adorned with jewelry of their own. Cartier created such a splash with Jeanne Toussaint's panthers that the big cat has become one of the store's trademark jewelry themes.

Enamel, diamond, and cabochon ruby panda bangle. (Courtesy David Webb)
Andrew Edgar

LEFT, *cabochon emerald–and–aquamarine starfish brooch by René Boivin. (Courtesy Fred Leighton)*
Andrew Edgar

RIGHT TOP, *polar-bear "good luck" clip of pavé diamonds, with a ruby eye. (Courtesy Van Cleef & Arpels, New York)*
Andrew Edgar

RIGHT MIDDLE, *beetle pin designed by Henryk Demner containing a cabochon sapphire (12.80 carats), a cabochon emerald (5.60 carats),*
sapphires (7.15 carats), emeralds (6.10 carats), and diamonds (7.20 carats). One of a kind.
Demner

RIGHT BOTTOM, *double-tiger bangle bracelet with yellow diamonds and black onyx. (Courtesy Cartier, New York)*
Andrew Edgar

OPPOSITE, *ruby, emerald, and diamond chameleon pin. Its cylindrical body rotates when the animal's tongue is depressed, allowing the colors to change from red to green,*
or in between. Signed by René Bovin. (Courtesy Fred Leighton, New York)
Andrew Edgar

The Plant Kingdom

One of the major design themes that has threaded its way from ancient civilizations to the present is the floral motif. The flower may comprise the entire jewel, take central place in a design, or form a background meant to set off a major stone. Flowers have been used in everything from tiaras to stomachers to create elegant as well as light and airy pieces. The types of flowers depicted—realistically or whimsically—are of uncounted variety.

Colored stones play a large part in creating lifelike flowers; and with increasingly sophisticated techniques, it has become possible to render flowers even more like the real thing. Some are created *en tremblant:* the flowers move when the wearer does. Another favored technique is the invisibly set jeweled flower, looking as if it blooms without the aid of a metal support. The invisible setting is frequently used by Van Cleef & Arpels, only one of many fine firms that favor floral designs. Seaman Schepps, Boucheron, and Tiffany & Co. are a few of many other companies associated with jeweled flowers.

Orchid brooch of diamonds set in 18-karat gold, with 10.06 carats of rubies in the center. (Courtesy Van Cleef & Arpels, New York)
Andrew Edgar

OPPOSITE, *rose pin with 21.83 carats of fancy, intense yellow diamonds. (Courtesy Van Cleef & Arpels)*
Andrew Edgar

ABOVE, *an amazing brooch with an almost hidden "throw-away" diamond, made in the '30s or '40s by Seaman Schepps. (Private collection)*
Fred Lyon

LEFT, *floral cluster formed of six flowerheads mounted* en tremblant *and decorated with round,*
pear-, marquise-, and baguette-shaped diamonds, signed by Tiffany & Co.
Copyright © 1988 Sotheby's, Inc.

RIGHT, *diamond flower pin by Neiman Marcus.*
Neiman Marcus

OPPOSITE, *magnificent diamond flower pin containing all flawless D-color diamonds weighing a total of 108.71 carats.*
Graff, London

John Traina's life is no less intriguing than the fascinating origins of the jewels he writes about. Born to noble Italian parents, he spent his childhood and youth traveling back and forth between Europe and the United States on the great luxury liners of the day: the *Rex,* the *Ile de France,* the *Liberté,* the *De Grasse*. His mother had a passion for fashion and jewels, and he observed her choices early on, while complaining bitterly at being included in her shopping ventures in New York, Paris, and Rome.

He was far more intrigued by the ships they traveled on, and after a graduate and undergraduate career at Stanford University, he began a lifelong career in shipping, which took him to the remotest corners of the world. Once an executive of passenger lines in South America and the Far East, he later went on to run both cruise and cargo ships, and started a new cruise line that opened up China. From his earliest youth, he traveled extensively in the Far East, the Pacific, North and South America, and Europe. He literally ran cruises around the world, and came to know countries and places that few people included in their travels.

John Traina is also a consummate collector. His years of traveling have brought fascinating treasures into his hands. He is a collector of antiques, Russian art, Easter Island art and statues, and antique automobiles, among other treasures he has found on his travels. And along with the more unlikely collections, he became intrigued with jewels and fine stones. He was able to find them in their countries of origin and was frequently asked to buy them for friends. In time, jewels became a real passion, as he bought sapphires in Thailand and Ceylon; rubies in Burma; rubies, emeralds, and sapphires in India; emeralds in Nepal and Colombia; semiprecious stones in Brazil; and pearls in Japan and the South Seas. In addition, he did some serious looking and shopping in Hong Kong and the major capitals of Europe. His trips to Africa brought him diamonds as well.

And from studying and acquiring magnificent stones, it was only a small leap to becoming intrigued by the major designers: Boucheron, Van Cleef, Tiffany, Verdura, Schlumberger, Picasso, Cartier, Belperron, Boivin, David Webb. Seeing what they did with the stones was a whole new field of interest, a lesson in design. And in recent times, watching the auctions and the major sales has sparked his interest as well.

John Traina is also one of the world's leading collectors of the works of the house of Fabergé, which he feels has given him an understanding of jewels as art.

He is a man of many interests, many facets, many contrasts. As a result of trips down the Amazon, and into the remoter spots in Africa and Nepal, he is as comfortable in the wilds as in the more civilized cities in this country and Europe. Not only does he love ships and the sea, he is equally enamored with jewels and their mysteries. He is also involved in consulting, investments, vineyards, the travel business, and writing. He has produced documentary films on unusual world destinations and published travel and exploration articles. And in spite of himself, he has become deeply enmeshed in his wife's international literary career, managing the foreign aspects in particular—in forty-nine countries, thirty-five languages—as well as television and film projects. He is a major factor in the vast organization they run, the juggling act that is business and family life today.

Traina has lived in San Francisco for much of his life, as well as in Europe, New York and Washington, D.C. He is the proud father of nine children, ranging in age from four to twenty-four, and the bemused owner of four dogs, a rabbit, three birds, and a potbellied pig.

"Coco."
Fred Lyon

Acknowledgments

My special thanks go to my researcher, Elizabeth Whelan Roman; photographers, Andrew Edgar, New York and Portsmouth, N.H., Fred Lyon, San Francisco, the late Jesse Gerstein, New York; and to those photographers who loaned us their new and unusual shots.

Additionally, I would very much like to thank the following people and organizations who generously contributed their time, knowledge, and resources to help with the completion of my book.

Sotheby's	Diana Scarisbrick	Humphrey Butler
Christie's	Michelle Atteyah	Janet Rosenthal
Nicola Bulgari	Faye Ifshin	Cri Cri Solak-Eastin
Edward J. Landrigan	Diamond Information Center	Tony Duquette
Stan Silberstein	Lillian Ostergard	John Faulder
Ronald Winston	Kevin Jenness	Nell Williams
William Chaney	François Mellerio	Julia Ogilvy
Nicolas Bongard	Florence Benagh	Brigitte Devine
Diane Dillon	James de Givenchy	National Geographic Society
Edward Asprey	Lisa Hubbard	Ronald Varney
Lincoln Foster	Charles Crederoli	Gwendoline Keywood
Gianmaria Buccellati	Morton Janklow	Charles Dishman
Angela Cummings	Ralph Destino	Marvin Newman
Denise De Luca	Gordon Roberts	Tony Coote
Stefan Hemmerle	Michel de Robert	Archduke Geza von Habsburg
Franz Hemmerle	Lynn Ramsey	Kenneth Snowman
Joel Rosenthal	Larry French	Nina Wahl
Pierre Jeannet	Bryan Cambridge	Carol Bohdan
Fred Leighton	Yone Akiyama	Caroline Dougherty
John Loring	Clare Sheppard	Mary Petriomonaco
Alain Boucheron	Vivian Katsanos	David Bennett
Jacques Bernard	Beatrice de Plinval	Alexandra Rhodes
Sidney Long	Pamela Harris	Marilyn Gibbons
Simon Teakle	Raymond Sancroft-Baker	Christopher Walling

Ann Getty
Mrs. Prentis Cobb Hale
Nan Kempner
Stan Roman
Jacqueline de Ribes
Marisa Berenson
Nancy Eisenbarth
Neil Letson
Jim Cheetham
Joel Wineroth
Joseph Wineroth
Bren Plaistow
Warren Cowan
Tiane C. Benson
Smithsonian Institution
Mrs. Carl Hahn

Howard Herzog
Alexander & Alexander of
    California, Inc.
Kim Des Marais
Stephen Magner
Fernanda Gilligan
Colleen Schmit
Alexandra Kindler
Monica Clark
Felice Lippert
Joseph Farish, Jr.
Audrey Friedman
Adriane Bishko
John Duff
Andrea DiNoto
Nancy Nicholas

Lisa Hamil
Lori Lipsky
Frances Jones
Henri Samuel
Frances & Sid Klein
Richard Buonomo
Janet Zappata
Carlo Ferrero Zendrini
Hans Stern
Sergio Baril
Leeann Karidis
Marguerite de Cerval
Marilu Klar
Philippe Arpels

Particular thanks go to François Curiel of Christie's and John Block of Sotheby's for their invaluable contribution to the book.

Bibliography

Accolade. "The Allure of Coloured Diamonds." November 1989: 26.

Arem, Joel E., Ph.D., F.G.A. *Color Encyclopedia of Gemstones.* 2d ed. New York: Van Nostrand Reinhold, 1987.

Auchincloss, Eve. "An Encore for Verdura." *Connoisseur,* June 1987.

Barracca, Jader, Giampiero Negretti, and Franco Nencini. *Le temps de Cartier.* Milan: Wrist International S.r.l., 1989.

Becker, Vivienne. *The Jewellery of René Lalique.* The Goldsmiths' Company, 1987.

Becker, Vivienne. "Schlumberger: A Look at His Life and Career." *Jewel* 1, no. 1 (1988): 28–37.

Bennet, David, and Daniela Mascetti. *Understanding Jewellery.* Suffolk, England: Antique Collectors' Club, 1990.

Black, J. Anderson. *The Story of Jewelry.* New York: William Morrow & Co., Inc., 1974.

Blauer, Ettagale. "The Fabulous '40s." *Art & Auction,* December 1989: 140–45.

Blauer, Ettagale. "Laurence Graff, London." *Art & Auction,* September 1987: 136–37.

Blauer, Ettagale. "The New Look." *Art & Auction,* December 1989: 142–45.

Breitling, Gunter, et. al. *Gold.* New York: Alpine Fine Arts Collection, Ltd., 1981.

Cartlidge, Barbara. *Les bijous au XXe siècle.* Paris: Payot, 1986.

Cavey, Christopher. *Gems & Jewels: Fact and Fable.* Secaucus, N.J.: Wellfleet Books, 1992.

Cerwinske, Laura. *Russian Imperial Style.* New York: Prentice Hall, 1990.

Collins, Amy Fine. "Schlumberger: More Than Elegant, Ravishing, and Chic." *Connoisseur,* July 1990.

Culme, John, and Nicholas Rayner. *The Jewels of the Duchess of Windsor.* New York: The Vendome Press in association with Sotheby's, 1987.

Cumming, Robert. *Christie's Guide to Collecting.* Englewood Cliffs, N.J.: Prentice-Hall, 1984.

Doubilet, David. "Australia's Magnificent Pearls." *National Geographic* 180, no. 6 (December 1991): 108–23.

Field, Leslie. *The Queen's Jewels: The Personal Collection of Elizabeth II.* New York: Harry N. Abrams, Inc., 1987.

Flamini, Roland. "Hot Stones." *Connoisseur,* May 1988.

Fogg, Georgia, and Louise Berg, eds. *Art at Auction: The Year at Sotheby's 1985–86.* New York: Sotheby's Publications, 1986.

Frégnac, Claude, et. al. *French Master Goldsmiths and Silversmiths from the Seventeenth to the Nineteenth Century*. New York: French & European Publications, Inc., 1966.

Gere, Charlotte. *American and European Jewelry: 1830–1914*. New York: Crown Publishers, Inc., 1975.

Gere, Charlotte. "Exquisite Inventions." *The Antique Collector* 61, no. 12 (December 1990): 66–69.

Gere, Charlotte, and Geoffrey C. Munn. *Artists' Jewellery: Pre-Raphaelite to Arts and Crafts*. Suffolk, England: Antique Collectors' Club, Ltd., 1989.

Gleason, Barbara, ed. *Notable Diamonds of the World*. New York: Diamond Promotion Service, NW Ayer Inc.

Hillier, Bevis. *Asprey of Bond Street: 1781–1981*. London: Quartet Books Limited, 1981.

Jacobson, Stuart E. *Only the Best: A Celebration of Gift Giving in America*. New York: Harry N. Abrams, Inc., 1985.

Jones, Proctor Patterson. *Napoleon: An Intimate Account of the Years of Supremacy, 1800–1814*. San Francisco: Proctor Jones Publishing Company, 1992.

Joyce, Kristin, and Shellei Addison. *Pearls: Ornament and Obsession*. New York: Simon & Schuster, 1993.

Kane, Robert E., et. al. "Rubies and Fancy Sapphires from Vietnam." *Gems & Gemology* 27, no. 3 (Fall 1991): 136–55.

Krashes, Laurence S. *Harry Winston: The Ultimate Jeweler*. 2d ed. Santa Monica, Calif.: Gemological Institute of America, 1986. 3d ed. New York: Harry Winston, Inc., 1988.

Letson, Neil. "The Peerless Verdura." *Connoisseur*, March 1983.

Loring, John. *Tiffany's One Hundred and Fifty Years*. Garden City, N.Y.: Doubleday & Co., Inc., 1987.

Manzari, Picci. "Preziosi riflessi di un epoca." *Capital*, December 1991.

Mascetti, Daniela, and Amanda Triossi. *Earrings: From Antiquity to the Present*. New York: Rizzoli International Publications, Inc., 1990.

Medina, Danny. "Nina Silberstein: A Designing Woman." *Trends* 5, no. 9 (October 1987): 18.

Melikian, Souren. "Dazzling Diamonds Send Prices Skyward." *International Herald Tribune*, 24 May 1988.

Menkes, Suzy. "The Golden Age of Designer Jewelry." *Connoisseur*, July 1990.

Menkes, Suzy. *The Royal Jewels*. 3d ed. London: Grafton Books, 1988.

Menkes, Suzy. *The Windsor Style*. Topsfield, Mass.: Salem House Publishers, 1988.

Morel, Bernard. *Les joyaux de la couronne de France*. Anvers: Fonds Mercator, 1988.

Nadelhoffer, Hans. *Cartier: Jewelers Extraordinary*. New York: Thames and Hudson, 1984.

Néret, Gilles. *Boucheron: Four Generations of a World-Renowned Jeweler*. New York: Rizzoli International Publications, Inc., 1988.

Newman, Harold. *An Illustrated Dictionary of Jewelry*. New York: Thames and Hudson, 1981.

Patch, S. S. *Blue Mystery: The Story of the Hope Diamond*. Washington, D.C.: Smithsonian Institution Press, 1976.

Porter, Bruce. "The Black Pearl Connection." *Connoisseur*, April 1991.

Proddow, Penny, and Debra Healy. *American Jewelry: Glamour and Tradition*. New York: Rizzoli International Publications, Inc., 1987.

Proddow, Penny, Debra Healy, and Marion Fasel. *Hollywood Jewels: Movies—Jewelry—Stars*. New York: Harry N. Abrams, Inc., 1992.

Purtell, Joseph. *The Tiffany Touch*. New York: Pocket Books / Simon & Schuster, 1973.

Quinn, Joan Agajanian. "Adornments: The Story of Seaman Schepps." Interview with Patricia Vaill. *Interview* 16, no. 5 (May 1986).

Raulet, Sylvie. *Art Deco Jewelry*. New York: Rizzoli International Publications, Inc., 1985.

Raulet, Sylvie. *Jewelry of the 1940s and 1950s*. New York: Rizzoli International Publications, Inc., 1988.

Raulet, Sylvie. *Van Cleef & Arpels*. New York: Rizzoli International Publications, Inc., 1987.

Scarisbrick, Diana. *Ancestral Jewels: Treasures of Britain's Aristocracy*. New York: The Vendome Press, 1990.

Scarisbrick, Diana. "Flocking Back to Verdura." *Departure*, September/October 1989.

Scarisbrick, Diana. "Wit on the Grand Scale." *Country Life*, 7 June 1990.

Schumann, Walter. *Gemstones of the World*. New York: Sterling Publishing Co. Inc., 1977.

Snowman, A. Kenneth, ed. *The Master Jewelers*. New York: Harry N. Abrams, Inc., 1990.

Tait, Hugh, *Jewelry: 7,000 Years*. New York: Harry N. Abrams, Inc., 1987.

Untracht, Oppi. *Jewelry: Concepts and Technology*. Garden City, N.Y.: Doubleday & Co., Inc., 1982.

Vincent, Steven. "Diamonds in the Rough." *Art & Auction* 14, no. 7 (February 1992): 78–85.

Ward, Fred. "Emeralds" *National Geographic* 178, no. 1 (July 1990): 38–69.

Ward, Fred. "Rubies and Sapphires" *National Geographic* 180, no. 4 (October 1991): 100–25.

Wheaton, Kathleen. "The Many-Faceted Mr. Stern." *Town & Country* March 1990.

White, John Sampson. "The Nation's Gem Collection: One Hundred Years." Scientific abstract,

Department of Mineral Sciences, National Museum of Natural History, Smithsonian Institution, 1986.

White, John Sampson, and Mary T. Winters. "George IV's Blue Diamond." *Lapidary Journal*, December 1991.

Willsberger, Johann. *Gold*. Garden City, N.Y.: Doubleday & Co., Inc., 1976.

Zucker, Benjamin. *Gems and Jewels: A Connoisseur's Guide*. New York: Thames and Hudson, 1984.